SELL Y

To MARK

[signature: Bryan McC...]

15/09/10   -019

SELL YOUR SELF!

Act Your Way To Sales Success!

BRYAN McCORMACK

First Published In Great Britain 2010
by www.BookShaker.com

Cover Design & Illustrations Bryan McCormack

CONTENTS

ACT ONE - ACTING & SELLING

ACT TWO - SELLING & ACTING

PRAISE

"This fast-moving, entertaining book is loaded with great ideas you can use immediately to increase your sales."
Brian Tracy, Self Improvement Expert, Speaker and Bestselling Author of 'The Psychology of Selling', www.briantracy.com

"Any person applying the advice, tips and tactics from 'Sell Your Self' will close more sales and build some great relationships – an excellent book."
Richard Denny, Motivational Speaker and International Bestselling Author of 'Selling to Win', www.denny.co.uk

"AT LAST! Someone who understands the importance of 'Acting and Presenting' in the SALES arena. As an Actor and Presenter I feel this book should be OBLIGATORY for anyone wanting to sell, act or present."
Paul Lavers, Actor and Presenter, www.paullavers.com

"This book will give you a decisive edge when you need to gain trust, influence decision makers and convince people that they really need what you've got. Applying tools and systems from acting to the role of selling, Bryan helps sales professionals at all levels get from the B-list to the A-list. If you want to be a star sales person this book is a must-read."
Simon Hazeldine, International Speaker, Business Performance Consultant and Bestselling Author of 'Bare Knuckle Selling' and 'Bare Knuckle Negotiating', www.simonhazeldine.com

"Packed full of strategies and techniques that you simply won't find anywhere else. Reading Bryan's tips will help anyone overcome their fear of rejection."
Michael Lee, Professional Copywriter and Author of 'How To Be An Expert Persuader', www.20daypersuasion.com

"Packed with good, solid advice that entertains as much as it illuminates. The style is warm and witty throughout making it a pleasure to spend time with the author, but that pleasure is deceptive, because while you are laughing you are also learning."

Stuart Palmer, Columnist for 'Writing Magazine',
www.writersnews.co.uk and www.alteredvistas.co.uk

ACT ONE &
BEGINNERS PLEASE!

1. INT. THE THEATRE. OPENING NIGHT

The AUDIENCE are arriving, finding their seats. The TV CAMERAS are in position. The atmosphere is ELECTRIC, lots of excited chat. Then, from the Public Address System:

ANNOUNCER: Good evening Ladies and Gentlemen and a very warm welcome to tonight's performance of, "Sell Your Self: Act Your Way To Sales Success", which will commence in the main auditorium shortly. Please take your seats.

2. INT. CONTROL GALLERY.

The TV DIRECTOR checks his Shooting Script.

Ok, stand by Studio. Ready to go Live.

3. INT. DRESSING ROOM.

Our Hero is making his final preparations. Then from the TANNOY on the wall:

TANNOY VOICE: Act One & Beginners please. Act One & Beginners to the stage. Mr McCormack, this is your Call. Good luck everyone.

Our Hero stands, ready to face his audience. With a last look in the mirror, he EXITS

4. INT. THE WINGS.

Our Hero ENTERS and presses the Call Button on the wall, signalling to the Stage Manager that he is in position.

5. INT. THE THEATRE.

The AUDIENCE are settling themselves. The LIGHTS in the auditorium begin to DIM. An excited air of ANTICIPATION!

6. INT. THE WINGS.

The Cue Light turns GREEN and Our Hero walks onstage to THUNDEROUS APPLAUSE!

And - Camera One!

THANK YOU! THANK YOU!

Members of the Academy, this award doesn't just belong to me – oh, sorry. Wrong introduction! Ahem...

There is one person more than any other that I really do need to thank.

He's the one who actually had the idea for this book in the first place.

It all began innocently enough. We were stood outside the pub. Sunday, September 27th 2009. About eight o'clock. Slight chance of rain...

Earlier in the day he had watched me interview another actor onstage as part of one of those, "An Afternoon With..." type events. He knew I was an actor myself - and that when I wasn't working as an actor I worked in sales. Although we'd known each other socially for nearly a year it was the first time he'd actually seen me 'perform' in front of an audience.

He told me he thought the interview went very well, which was nice of him. He complimented me on how I managed to relax the interviewee whilst at the same time engaging the audience. What a very nice man this chap is, I thought. Then all of a sudden - look out lads, here it comes – he turned to me and said:

"Do you think you could write a book?"

Ladies and Gentlemen, here he is – the man whose 'light bulb' moment it was that resulted in the book you are about to read - [You may as well, you've paid for it!] It gives me great pleasure to introduce to you the *very nice man* himself –

Ok, stand by Studio. We are going to the Foreword...

...who has also, incidentally, written the Foreword - please put your hands together for The One! The Only! Rintu Basu!

And... Cue Rintu!

FOREWORD

I am a very privileged guy. I witnessed the birth of two great books. The first was one that happened only in my head. The second and far better book is the one you are holding in your hands.

Last September standing outside a pub in Glasgow with Bryan the idea for this book started taking shape (he seems to think it was my idea but I think he must take the lion's share of the blame). I know nothing really about acting but as we discussed how acting related to sales I could see a lot of potential.

I imagined a great sales book. With new perspectives, ideas and techniques. What if you as a sales person could learn to:

- have the charisma of a screen legend

- work an audience to a frenzy of excitement

- take on the characteristics of a great sales person

- tell the story of your product or service in an entertaining and engaging way

This would be a book worth reading. I imagined the whole thing in my head and encouraged Bryan to write it.

But as with most things, reality and imagination are not the same. Bryan went away and wrote his book instead. The one that is in your hands right now. Does it contain all the things I imagined? Actually it does and in a far more witty and imaginative way than I expected. But there is something more than just these ideas going on.

I was not expecting a personal development manual. The ideas Bryan espouses reach further than just acting or just sales. Hidden in these pages are gems that apply to all walks of life. As you read further into this book just notice how much you can apply to every area of your life not just your selling ability. This is pure self development from an actor's perspective and applied to sales. Never in a million years could I have imagined that.

Will this book dramatically increase your sales, change your life, make you rich and famous? No, only you can do that...but if you want real concrete advice on how to go about all of that then the advice in this book is phenomenal.

I am a very privileged guy. I witnessed the birth of two great books. You have the better of the two in your hands.

Rintu Basu, Author,
'Persuasion Skills Black Book',
www.thenlpcompany.com

BEFORE WE BEGIN...

…let me tell you what this book is **not** going to do for you!

This book is **not** going to teach you how to sell, it is **not** going to give you the confidence to sell and it is **not** going to help motivate you to sell.

Oh and don't look for any of that stuff on 'Presentation Skills' either. If that's what you're looking for, this is **not** the book for you!

And why not? Two reasons. One, there are a multitude of great books out there already that can impart those things to you. That's **not** what this book is about. This book is different to any other sales book you have ever read before.

Two, the fact that you've bought this book tells me that you already have those skills. What you want to learn is how I can help you to not only improve those skills and make them more effective but more importantly, use them better than anyone else, correct?

You want to know what it is that almost always makes an actor a better seller than you, don't you? You want to know what it is that an actor like me knows about the secrets of consistently successful selling that you don't, yes?

And above all, you want practical ways in which **you** can use **my** skills to help **you** sell more of your product, not how to make a speech or how not to make a complete arse of yourself in front of the bigwigs from head office. Correct?

Well that's good, no scrub that - that's great! But why settle for second best? Instead of me just helping you to sell better, let's work together to transform you into The Best Seller That You Can Be, how does that sound? Agreed? Yes? Fantastic! And let me tell you now, simply by buying this book you have potentially improved your chances of beating the opposition by a good 50%. So give yourself a pat on the back - that was a smart move and one that I promise you will not regret!

So now - let me tell you what this book **will** do for you!

This book **will** show you why actors often make the best sales people, it **will** teach you the skills they have that you don't [skills that you need!] and with it you **will** learn secrets that will give you the edge over your competitors. Competitors that you will leave behind, coughing in the dust you've kicked up as you race away from them on the road to success!

So go ahead and congratulate yourself on your sharp investment!

This unique book shows why actors nearly always make the best sellers and if you are serious about being a real success in sales there is a lot that you can learn from them. Follow the programme as outlined in this book and you too will soon be a sales superstar!

When not working as an actor, I have always worked in 'proper jobs' where I knew I could use my acting skills. I knew that by doing jobs that involved interaction with customers, I could not only keep myself sharp, but I would also be getting:

1. great material for future scripts
   [and books like this!]
2. characters that I could play in the future

Over the past twenty years, in my 'proper jobs', I have worked for:

- A major UK supermarket
  [that's customer service covered]

- A national rail company
  [so I know all about dealing with complaints!]

- A leading high street electrical retailer
  [face to face selling and upselling]

- Call centres, both inbound and outbound
  [and that's distance selling covered too!]

Which is what makes this book so special - unlike a lot of the sales books out there, in this case the author has actually done some selling! I've seen the world of work from both sides, as a trade unionist/shop steward and as a manager. My first ever selling gig was to try and convince the staff in the supermarket where I worked to join the Shopworker's Union!

Since the age of eight, I have spent my entire life in front of audiences of one kind or another, either making speeches at conferences and hustings, chairing meetings, doing presentations, running training courses, as well as working as an actor on stage and in television and radio. In this book we're talking specifically about acting skills as selling tools, but the truth is that you can use them in almost any area of life, as you will see…

And yes I've made mistakes. I'll even admit to some of them as we go along to help you avoid making them too!

So this is what we're going to do.

I'm going to start off by talking a bit about what you think you know about acting and the truth about acting. This is an important foundation for all that follows - you'll never be able to effectively apply the acting skills secrets I'm going to give you if you don't have an appreciation of what actors are all about and how they do what they do. And why.

Then I'm going to demonstrate why my acting skills will, more often than not, make an actor like me a better seller than even a superior salesperson like you. But don't worry, I'll be teaching you those same skills so that by the end of the book you'll know nearly as much as I do!

Finally I'll give you some practical steps that you can take to apply what you've learned from me, along with examples of how I used what I knew – that my competitors didn't – to my advantage.

Oh, and one last thing – by way of thanks for all you're going to learn – do us a favour, eh? Remember to point them to this book when they ask you how you did it!

Bryan McCormack is the author of this book. He was born in Ayr, Scotland on Friday the 29th of April 1966 and started performing at the age of 8. He gained his Equity Card with Cumbernauld Theatre Company in 1987 at the age of 21. For this he is eternally grateful to Stage Manager Bill Winter and Artistic Director Robert Robson. Writing this book – at the age of 43 – has changed his life and reading it could change yours too!

SELL YOUR SELF!

Act Your Way To Sales Success!

BRYAN McCORMACK

ACT ONE -
ACTING & SELLING

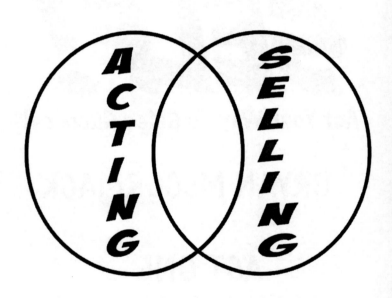

CHAPTER ONE

CURTAIN UP!

In this initial chapter I'm going to give you your first insights into why actors make such good sales people and why you need to learn what they already know in order to maximise your potential as a Super Seller.

Actors. There's A Lot of Them About...

Ok, let me start by asking you this question - how much time do you spend watching stuff, like television, in a day? On average. Two, three hours, maybe more? That's about twenty hours a week, over a thousand hours a year. Add in the number of times you go to the cinema or watch a DVD or Blu-Ray and you could easily add on half as much again. Have you got a favourite TV show that you never miss an episode of? If so, then that number could go even higher. And all the time you're sat in front of that screen, you're doing one thing more than anything else. Can you guess what it is? You got it - watching actors!

There's No Escaping Escapism!

Stop and think for a moment how many times during a day you see actors at work. For instance, where would talk shows be without them? But even outside of TV and the movies there are many other moments during your day when actors and what they do will cross your path. How about all the commercials that you see between those TV shows you watch? They're full of…? Actors. If you have video clips on your mobile, most of them will probably feature…? Actors. If you go online to your favourite show's Official Website what will you see…? Actors.

Think about the world of advertising and how many products are promoted by…? Actors. Whether it's on TV, at the movies, in magazines, online or on the radio [more about that in a minute], realise that the advertising you are surrounded by is not all posed by models, many of them are…? You're way ahead of me, I can tell.

So now you are beginning to realise just how much of your time is spent being influenced by actors and their performances and that you see actors in more places than you might think. But don't forget that you also hear them too. And it's not just the DJs - on talk radio or music stations - and the commercials between the songs where you can find them, oh no.

Let's Talk Radio!

If you listen to radio drama - or comedy - then everything you hear is being performed by…? Actors. If you like to listen to audio books then they are being read by…? Actors. And what about all those cartoons and CGI animated movies you watch too? Who are they voiced by…? Actors.

And finally, when you play your favourite console games, the voices you hear are those of…

Actors. You see 'em, you hear 'em - they're everywhere!

And if you think about it, you could be spending more time with certain actors than you do with certain members of your own family! [Which, if yours is anything like mine, is not necessarily such a bad thing!] But what do you know about these people? What's your perception of them and what they do? And what the heck does it have to do with selling anyway? All will be revealed, but first...

Why Acting Skills Matter To Sellers

So we've realised that every day we are surrounded by actors and what they do, often without being aware of it. But why does that matter and what is its relevance to Selling?

Actors are arguably the most consistently admired, looked up to, lived through and interesting and interested-in people in our modern media-based society. Because of the nature of their profession, and the means by which it promotes its products, Actors know more about the business of selling than many sellers do. And that's what you're here to learn, right?

Ok then, let me show why this is so important to you as a seller with this very simple exercise.

The Seller Sells The Sale

Think about your favourite actor. Now, in your mind's eye, imagine that actor selling what you sell to your customers. Picture him doing your job.

He's doing exactly what you do, only it's him that's doing it and not you. He's selling what you sell to the same customers that you sell to but you're not selling your product, he is.

He may be pointing out the same features and benefits that you do, but it's him that's doing it, not you. Think how he would go about it. Can you picture him doing that? Okay, now answer the following questions:

1. What is the probability of them making a sale? High or Low?

2. What are the chances that people would still buy from them if they didn't know who they were? High or Low?

3. If they were selling over the phone, would they be more or less likely to make a sale?

4. What are the chances that the public would rather buy from them than from you? High or Low?

If you are in any doubt as to the answers to those questions, then let me strongly suggest that you go and get your refund now. You are obviously either:

- someone who bought the wrong book or

- someone who really shouldn't be in Sales. Goodbye and good luck in your new career!

For the rest of the class, one final question:

5. What is it that they are doing that you're not? Hmm?

There are only really two possible answers to that question.

1. The first is that they are saying things that you are not saying, things that are turning prospects into customers more effectively than whatever your current spiel is.

2. The second is that they are saying the same things that you are saying, but in a different way, a way that turns prospects into customers more effectively than whatever your current style of delivery is.

For most of the sellers I have come across, both those statements are equally true. So how do you learn to say the right things in the right way?

Easy - keep reading!

Why Selling Skills Matter To Actors

Actors need selling skills even more than sellers need acting skills. In fact, as we go I will prove to you that an actor who is a poor salesman won't be an actor for long, at least not professionally and successfully.

An actor must always be a good promoter of the show that he's in and also often of himself, depending on the kind of actor he is. The global entertainment industry is a market constantly in search of new product, particularly now in these multi-channel days of time-shifting viewing.

I have watched over the years as careers in entertainment have become shorter, clubs and theatres have closed and the medieval bear-pit has been resurrected as the modern-day TV talent show, in all its unashamed cruelty. We no longer have all-round entertainers such as Bruce Forsyth who, whatever your personal opinion of him, is a showman of some considerable skill. Today we have semi-talented innocents who get to do their party piece in public. And when we ask if they can do anything else the answer is always no, not really.

Product Placement

Many of our modern society's so-called 'celebrities' are little more than talent-lite entertainment products, no less manufactured than many of the boy bands of the 1990s. Tabloid editors love them as long as their antics continue to interest the public, but when their star fades and they come to the end of their limited synthetic lifespan, the journalistic wolf-pack will turn on them for one final feast. Having charted - and often colluded in - the minor celebrity's rise to fame they now engage equally energetically in engineering their fall. And then it's onto the latest piece of fresh meat for the media mincing machine...

And all the while, waiting in the wings, trained actors and professional entertainers watch out for the day when the execs finally realise that reality TV is finished. Because there's nobody left to exploit.

ESP

The entertainment industry is an ESP type business, contributing around 8% of GDP in the UK. An ESP business is one where:

EVERYONE SELLS A PRODUCT

Keep that thought in mind as we go through the rest of this chapter. There are more products to be sold than just the ones you sell and this knowledge is a vital addition to your Seller's Toolkit.

What is a Product?

A product is anything that there is as market for, anything that you can sell, anything that people are prepared to buy, anything that can make you enough money to make selling it worth doing. That's not what a product does though. What a product does and what a product is are two totally different things.

What Does a Product Do?

A product does one of two things and can be one of two types. It can either be a MAN type product which means it:

MEETS A NEED

or it can be an SAP type product which means it:

SOLVES A PROBLEM

So let's get going on this journey into meeting needs and solving problems and show all you sellers why acting skills are the selling tools that you need, shall we?

Homework

Okay, your homework for Chapter 2 - yes, homework, don't look so shocked, we agreed to work together to make you into The Best Seller You Can Be, remember? So that means you need to do your share too. Your homework is to sit yourself down in front of the TV with a notebook and watch QVC for an hour. See, that wasn't so hard, was it!

I want you to observe the presenter and learn from them. Note down anything they do that you find really effective, that you think you could use in your next sales opportunity. Jot down any phrases they use that you think work and pay attention to the way they say what they say, their tone of voice, pace and emphasis. Note too if what they do changes how you feel about the product by the time they move on to the next one and most important of all - would you now buy it? A word of advice though, try and do this exercise without having your credit card handy!

COMING UP IN CHAPTER 2...

We get our first insights into the world of the actor and a brief history of acting. Bryan shows us that there are only two kinds of actor and unveils the first important parallels between acting and selling. See you there!

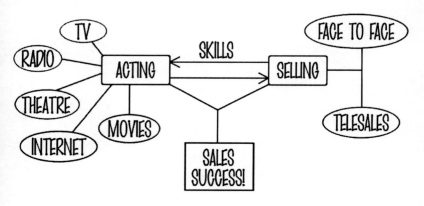

Bryan McCormack

CHAPTER TWO

AN ACTOR'S LIFE FOR...YOU?

Hello and welcome back to chapter 2. Hands up anybody who didn't do their homework… Now if you did go and watch QVC, what did you see? You would have seen the kind of rapport skills that you need being used to outstanding effect. If you were really on the ball you would have closed your eyes and just listened. You would then have heard the kind of skills that you need being used to succeed where you currently fail.

Remember the exercise where I had you picture your favourite actor selling your product for you? Run that scenario again but now imagine The Queen Bee of QVC UK herself, Julia Roberts, [no, not that one] selling your product for you. How do you think she would do compared to you?

What Do You Know?

Acting in particular and performing in general involves lots of different skills which, as I will show you later, are applicable to selling. But before we come to that, stop and think about what you actually know about the acting profession. I mean, what you actually know for yourself that you have actually experienced yourself.

Forget what you've read about actors in those magazine interviews or heard them say to the chat show hosts. You may have read their autobiography and gained an insight into their life as a result but what do you actually know for yourself about what it takes to be an actor or a performer of any kind in front of an audience?

Getting Started

I started performing at the age of eight. I was born and bred in the Scottish seaside town of Ayr and since Ayrshire is famously 'The Land O' Burns' [Robert Burns, poet and probably the most internationally well-known Scot after Sean Connery and Billy Connolly] the local schools would hold an annual Burns Poetry recitation competition, which I won at the first attempt. Sadly the blue certificate of merit I got [the first of three I won at school] has long since been lost, but it was then that I realised that performing in general, and acting in particular, was what I wanted to do with my life.

It was about this time that it dawned on me that actors are people who get to spend their time pretending to be other people and getting paid for it.

My young brain quickly deduced that this meant there was a chance that when I grew up I could spend my time pretending to be Doctor Who, my favourite childhood TV character. Now there was an incentive to a career as an actor if ever there was one!

Bitten by The Acting Bug!

It soon became increasingly clear to everyone, including my parents, that I had a natural talent for performing. My Christmas and birthday presents consisted solely of things like ventriloquist's dummies, puppet theatres, marionettes, magician's sets and all sorts of other performance related stuff including books on acting and actors. [And here I am all these years later writing one of my own!]

At primary school back in the 1970s, as well as being in the school choir, every school play and doing the Bible readings for weekly assembly and end of term services, I was always organising shows for my philistine classmates using those presents. On the one hand this had the effect of making me temporarily popular with said classmates as it meant they got time off lessons to watch me learning how to entertain an audience. On the other hand, it made me terribly unpopular when I got time off lessons to go do my shtick for another class while they carried on doing maths and English without me. Oh, the trials of a life on the stage!

At secondary school it was more of the same. There I had a wonderful drama teacher, an elderly spinster by the name of Doris Paul. Miss Paul, as she was known, was a great encouragement and my first mentor. She was the first person to help me harness, develop and direct my talent and for that I'll always be grateful to her.

Turning Professional

After that it was various local Amateur Dramatic Societies [more about them later] in various locations as the family moved around a bit. Finally, in late 1982 I found myself in Cumbernauld, 13 miles north of Glasgow and in January 1983 went along to the Youth Theatre for the first time.

Cumbernauld Theatre was where I first encountered proper actors and theatre professionals. The Youth Theatre, under John Haswell, was a great training ground and Cumbernauld Theatre at the time, in the early/mid 1980s was a very special place. It was one of the happiest times of my life and I wouldn't have missed it for the world!

So what is an Actor?

The simplest definition of an actor that I can think of is someone who pretends to be someone else.

There are essentially two kinds of actor - The Character Actor and The Personality Actor. Let's look at the differences between them both:

THE CHARACTER ACTOR [that's me, hello!] is the kind of actor who loves to change the way they look, the way they walk, talk, everything. He tries to get as far away from himself as possible to create a believable character. Peter Sellers was a classic example of this kind of actor. A modern day equivalent would be Jim Carey.

THE PERSONALITY ACTOR on the other hand is the kind favoured by Hollywood. No matter what they're in, they always look the same and sound the same. Every character they play is a version of themselves. Sean Connery was a classic example of this kind of actor. And there are hundreds, if not thousands, of others you could think of today.

So thinking about the actors you like and admire, which category do they fall into? Character or personality?

What is it that attracts you to them and their performance? We'll come back to this in a later chapter. But before that I need to give you...

A [Very] Brief History of Acting

The very least you need to know is this:

1. Acting, Performing and Theatre goes all the way back to the Ancient Greeks, or so they say.

2. There's this really famous Elizabethan bloke called Billy Shakespeare, you're bound to have heard of him - wrote loads of dead famous plays like Harry 5, Dickie 3, Alfa Romeo and Juliet, King Leer, all that lot.

3. Laurence Olivier was perhaps the most famous ac-tohr of the late twentieth century. Coming a close second were two baldy blokes called John Feelgood and Ralph Richardson [Collectively known as The Three Stooges - Johnny, Larry and Ralphie].

4. Apparently acting as we know it today only started in the early part of the twentieth century, between the two world wars. I say 'apparently' because I wasn't there at the time.

5. There were these two Russian blokes called Stannis and Lavsky. Or maybe it was one bloke called Stan Lavsky, I'm not sure. Anyway, he's regarded as the top notch guy for teaching realism in acting as opposed to the pantomime stuff that was the norm before. Again, apparently.

After that it's pretty much all movie stars, sitcoms and soaps and 'celebrities' [Gawd 'elp us...]

And that's about it really. See, told you it was brief! Moving on...

Stanislavsky & Strasberg

OK, so after that - not entirely serious - brief history, let's zero in on this bloke Stanislavsky. Stan The Man is a major figure in the history of acting and his ideas on what acting should be like for an audience and how actors should actually act, still influence the profession today. But who is he? And there's another chap to consider as well - Lee Strasberg, famously of The Actor's Studio in New York. Heard of either of them? No? Not to worry. You're about to!

So This Stanislavsky Bloke. Who's He Then?

Born in 1863, [the year his predecessor Mikhail Shchepkin died] Konstantin Sergeyevich Stanislavsky was a member of the Moscow Art Theatre in the 1920s. Building on what Shchepkin had begun before him, his approach, revolutionary at the time, was to see acting as something that should be realistic instead of a big, loud, over the top, 'hammy' pantomime type performance. Instead of an audience being entertained they were to be a fly on the invisible fourth wall.

Helped and undoubtedly influenced by the plays of one Anton Chekov, what Stanislavsky came up with, his methods of teaching acting and how actors should implement them, was called The System. [From now on

I'm going to call him Stan as it saves on both the typing and the ink.]

There's been a lot of rot talked about Stan in particular and acting in general over the years by people who have a vested interest in making it seem more complicated than it is. Acting isn't difficult to do, but it is easy to do badly and hard to do well. More on that later...

Stanislavsky's System & Strasberg's Method

Stan's initial idea was what is termed 'emotional memory'. Basically, if your character has to feel sad, you don't just pretend to be sad, you think of a sad moment in your own life and channel the resultant emotion you feel into your performance. The whole idea was that an actor should be as truthful and realistic as he could. [Which is a bit of an irony when you consider that acting is all about pretending to be something you're not!]

At the same time as Stan was doing his shtick in Moscow, over in the USA between the wars there was an acting company known as The Group Theatre. It comprised some big acting names you've never heard of like Stella Adler, Sanford Meisner and Howard Clurman.

They got wind of what Stanislavsky was up to in Russia and a guy named Lee Strasberg came up with his own version called The Method. Lee S is best known for being head of The Actor's Studio in New York, which has produced a whole bucket load of Method Actors, some Very Big Names in Hollywood among them.

Head & Heart - Two Approaches

Some describe acting as a combination of intellect and instinct. I prefer to think of it as a combination of intellect and emotion, not quite the same thing. If acting is about realism, as Stan The Man said it should be, then you need to find the right combination of those two things that feels real and suits the character you're playing.

Since there are only two kinds of actor, that means there are only two approaches you can take to acting:

1. You play the character as written on the page. He looks the same and sounds the same as the real you. You play out the character's actions in the script as if he was a version of you.

2. You create the character you find written on the page. He looks and sounds different to the real you. You use your imagination to find out:

   a. how you think he would react to what happens in the script and

   b. create and map out that character's back-story prior to the events of the play.

These two fundamental approaches are very important for later on, but don't worry, we'll come back to them in the second half of the book. For the moment, all you need to remember is this vitally important fact:

Acting is a Business

I am in the business of acting, you are in the business of selling. If selling is your business, you need certain key skills at a certain level of ability in order to survive, make a half-decent living and eventually 'make it'. If on the other hand, acting is your business, then you need the same thing in a different way as we shall see in the next chapter.

The selling business sells three basic products - services, goods and essentials. The entertainment business also sells three basic products - literary works, audio and visual works and one other that is unique to the world of showbusiness. Actors themselves.

Parallel Worlds

In the selling world there are certain big names - such as Brian Tracy, to name one - who are as well known as the products they sell, which are usually their accumulated wisdom, insight and expertise. In the acting world, there are certain big names who, in Hollywood parlance, are known as 'openers' - actors who can open a film simply by being in it. People like Will Smith, Tom Cruise, Clint Eastwood, Eddie Murphy etc. They are so popular that people will go to see them, not the movie.

As a seller, how would you like people to buy your product, without knowing what it is, simply because it's You that's selling it! Nice work if you can get it!

People like this, in these parallel worlds of selling and acting, have one thing in common - they have a loyal fan base built on their reputation for customer service, brand recognition and product quality. Sound familiar?

Homework

Your homework for chapter three is to get a blank sheet of paper and split it into two halves marked Actors and Acting. Write down everything you can think of that relates to both subjects. Then we'll see how much a seller like you knows about the world of an actor like me!

COMING UP IN CHAPTER 3...

Bryan gives us a personal glimpse of an actor's life and shows us how to deal with the greatest enemy of both actors and sellers - Fear.

See you there!

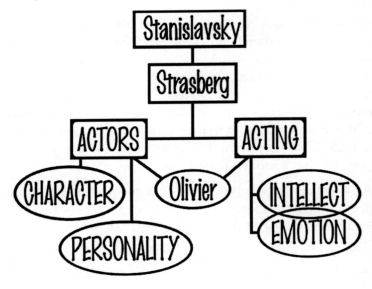

CHAPTER THREE

ACTING & SELLING 101

Actor For Sale!

Actors are employees, just like anyone else in the world of work. And to find work, they have to do the same things that sellers like you do.

You go for job interviews, they go for auditions.

You go for a permanent position, they are all on temporary contracts.

You sell a product, they sell a product.

You want to be promoted, they want to famous.

You are judged on your performance - and so are they!

Acting? Well it's, er...

Acting, at its simplest, is the business of pretending to be someone else. But as I'm sure you're thinking to yourself right now, there must be more to it than that? And you'd be right, there is. I don't want to get too far ahead of ourselves but for now think on this:

How good do you think you have to be to be able to earn a living from acting? Or at the very least, a decent second income? What's the real difference between two people, both of whom can act but only one of them gets paid for it? What do you think the answer is?

Well keep thinking about it and I will tell you later!

There's No Business Like...

...Showbusiness, that's for sure. But sadly it's no longer the business of putting on shows. Like the music industry before it, the product itself is no longer the primary focus but the potential profit that can be made from it is. Nick Drake made some of the most beautiful music you'll ever hear but it's not commercial and if he were alive today and trying for a record deal, he wouldn't stand a chance. He'd have to put it up on the internet himself in order to get it heard. The drive for commercial profit over artistic quality impoverishes us all and our culture is all the coarser for it. But, like it or not, the modern-day entertainment industry is geared away from all artistic endeavour and towards commercialism, profitability and success. Ethel Merman wouldn't recognise the place.

What do Sellers know about Acting?

Acting is a job. Just like selling is a job. As a seller you will know that, as far as your Team Leader or Regional Manager is concerned, you are only as good as your last day's performance against your Sales Target. Well an actor is just the same - he is only ever as good as his last performance too! And every time he gets a gig, there's always that nagging thought that this gig may well be his last. One day it will be.

Houston, We Have A Problem...

It always puzzles me when I read about how, for the majority of people, apparently the idea of public speaking fills them with dread. I'll be honest with you, it's something I find hard to relate to as I've never been intimidated by the idea of standing up in front of any size of audience and doing my shtick.

Even during those periods where I've been out of work for a while, when I do get another job, I can't wait to get back out there! Seriously, it's like I come alive when I'm out there. It doesn't frighten me, never has. Never will. Being in front of an audience is as natural to me as breathing.

...A Presentation Problem!

Yet for most people, no matter how outgoing their personality, the idea of having to do a presentation seems to fill them with dread. I have seen super-confident managers who could manage a team of sales agents with their eyes shut reach for the brown trousers at the very idea. And the reason why is really simple. It's not the nerves themselves. It's not lack of knowledge about the subject. It's not even the fear of making a fool of themselves as such. It's the self-inflicted mental torture that is -

The Nightmare Scenario

...Of "What If Something Goes Wrong?" It's being caught out by The Big Boss asking a question they can't answer or worse, knowing the answer but forgetting it under pressure. It's the projector breaking down and having to work from notes that you neglected 'cos you spent hours working on your fancy PowerPoint instead. Some people can indeed be the agents of their own downfall. I'll come to that in a minute.

Facing Your Fears

Just in case you missed it the first time round, or if you think I'd forgotten, let me reiterate that this book is not the place to find out how to face your fears and make presentations. Sorry, I can't help you. I just can't relate to that - but then again I was the weird kid who was never frightened by Doctor Who. I have never hidden behind a sofa in my life - I was always on the edge of my seat!

Although I've never been intimidated by standing up in front of people, I have been afraid of different things at different times in my life, of course I have. Much less now though, because I've learned by experience how to deal with my fear. So the general principles of overcoming fear, yes, I can help you with but the specifics of standing up in front of people, no.

Fear is simply negative expectation, the opposite of faith if you like. Faith isn't simply believing in something, it's much more than that. Faith is earnest, confident, intense expectation of something good. You have to admit, that's a much more powerful definition than simply believing in something, which often is nothing more than mental assent. Fear is just...

Faith In Reverse

...An earnest, confident, intense expectation of something bad. And since people always act on what they believe, then everything about the way you live will conform to and confirm what you believe, good or bad. If you are afraid that you will die in a plane crash, then that fear will stop you from flying. If you are afraid that you'll make a fool of yourself, then if that's what you expect to happen, guess what's likely to happen?

However, if, like an actor, you can learn to adopt a persona, then there's nothing to be afraid of as it's not You that does it. That's not to say there aren't dangers with this approach - I'm not suggesting that you become a complete fantasist - but if you've ever fallen victim to a con-man then you will know how effective adopting a persona can be.

I've learned to apply this principle to every area of my life, to the extent that nowadays I'm not intimidated by too much, even when I'm doing something new for the first time [like writing a book!] and I'll be showing you how you too can use this strategy effectively later in the book. But first...

Even I Make Mistakes

Just because I find it incredibly easy to walk out in front of an audience, please don't make the mistake of thinking that I was equally confident in every area of my life. I can assure you that I wasn't. Let me give you just one example - I was supremely confident when it came to performing but extremely intimidated when it came to chatting up women. Ironic isn't it.

You would think that I would have been able to use my acting skills to good effect when it came to girls, but no. Because I had a history of rejection as a child, as I grew up into a hormonally-charged teenager I had an intense expectation that I would be rejected. And because I expected it, I wasn't surprised when it happened. [I'll return to the subject of rejection in Chapter 15.]

So somehow I failed to make the connection and as a result it took me years to learn what I now know about adopting a character persona. It works for self-defence just as well as for selling and aren't you glad I'm potentially saving you years of frustration here!

But then sometimes it takes someone else to point out to you what's hidden in plain view. The solution to our problem is usually obvious to everyone except us! That's why you need other people in your life - connections - for true success. You cannot do it all on your own. [The power of connections is discussed in a later chapter.]

Homework

Your homework for chapter 4 is to split a sheet of paper into two columns. In the left-hand column, write down all the things you are now or have been afraid of that involve interaction with other people. If you're feeling really brave then add things that you haven't done yet but which you dread the idea of doing. In the second column write down the solutions you think my acting skills could give a seller like you to help you overcome those fears.

COMING UP IN CHAPTER 4...

Bryan gives us a basic introduction to acting and selling and we gain our first insights into how effectively the two fit together. See you there!

Bryan McCormack

CHAPTER FOUR

ACTING & SELLING 102

The late Barry Letts, producer of *Doctor Who* from 1970 to 1974 once said, "I'm a good actor but I'm simply not good at selling myself." That's the problem this book is intended to help you fix. One person who has no difficulty in promoting himself as a brand is Donald Trump...

Why I Love The Trumpster

Donald Trump, whatever your opinion of him, is a man who clearly understands the power of self-marketing. Some may find his habit of putting his name on everything distasteful, but do you think he cares?

I first came across The Trumpster late one night on BBC One when I stumbled across *The Apprentice USA*. It's now one of my favourite shows, mainly due to every episode being a masterclass on how not to screw up. There is something deeply satisfying about watching people who think they are so going to win blowing their chances right before your eyes - and not even realising that that's what they're doing. Love it!

Over the years I've been watching the show, I've noticed that there are a few clearly discernible types of sellers who seem to crop up time and again - and they're usually the first to bomb in the boardroom!

The Alienator

The Alienator is the one that nobody can get along with, the one who's so pushy that they tee off everyone around them. They are so arrogant and over confident that they are incapable of any subtlety or effective man management. They erroneously think that the force of their personality is enough to carry them through the task and ensure they impose their will on the rest of the team. They are always the last to see this, if at all, which is usually just after The Trumpster tells them that they're fired!

Hyperboy & Hypergirl

These two supposed Superhero Sellers are in fact nothing more than a couple of self-confidence tricksters. They are the ones who really big themselves up to be Top Banana At Selling Anything [they should really be Spin Doctors instead] only for them to crash and burn and display an Actualised Ability Rating of zero point zero zero whilst simultaneously hitting 101% on The BS Scale.

The Oddball

In every series there's always an oddball - a guy with a tenuous grasp of reality, a loner who has no idea of how to work as part of a team. He usually sulks when he doesn't get his own way and the other mean kids won't let him play with the toys. Nobody likes him, everybody wants The Trumpster to fire him, but nobody seems to have the smarts to make him Project Manager ASAP in order to get rid of him!

The producers of this show have very cleverly taken that most stressful of social interactions - the job interview - and ramped up the tension by throwing together an assortment of personalities and temperaments that they know will clash and make great television. Yet none of the willing lab rats seem to be savvy enough to recognise this subtle manipulation.

Bombing In The Boardroom!

The best part of the show is, of course, when the losing team are told to meet The Trumpster, "in the boardroom, where one of you will be fired!"

This is where the candidates do themselves the most harm, losing their temper, attacking and blaming each other and generally doing themselves no favours whatsoever. They are so determined to sabotage their rivals that they forget that The Trumpster is sitting there quietly, saying little or nothing, watching them kiss their dream job goodbye!

I've watched in amazement as candidates have torpedoed themselves by bringing the person they dislike back to the boardroom instead of the one who really flunked the test. Don't they realise that The Trumpster knows they are making an emotional decision instead of a business one? And why don't they understand that shooting your mouth off about someone else is a sure-fire way to get yourself fired instead? I mean, I've been watching this show for long enough and even I get that!

But what they and all the others who bomb in the boardroom have in common, and I've seen it time and again in my real-life selling career, is a lack of flexibility and an almost pathological inability to realise early enough that what they are doing isn't working. If only they had they could have changed their approach and potentially turned the situation around. But all too often they don't. And yes, I've been one of them!

When Things Go Wrong

When things go wrong is where you really start to see the underlying deficiencies in a seller's personality. The ability to recover from potential disaster is what makes performing at the same time both thrilling and terrifying for an actor. Throwing in an ad-lib that works, covers an error or better still gets a laugh, is an ability that not everyone will have the self-confidence to attempt, let alone the ability to actually pull off.

If only The Apprentice lab rats could realise that the best way to beat the competition is to do a basic SWOT analysis on both themselves, the task and their team mates. [If you are an actor, your future career could well depend on this sort of self-analysis!]

Wot's a SWOT?

A SWOT analysis is a basic business tool that is equally applicable to life outside the business arena. SWOT stands for:

STRENGTHS - what you're good at, better at and best at. Improve these.

WEAKNESSES - what you're not very good at. Strengthen these.

OPPORTUNITIES - showcases for your ability. Capitalise on these.

THREATS - people who are better than you. Eliminate these.

[Please don't take that last one literally!]

Those candidates trying for a job with The Trumpster who step up to the plate as Project Manager all make the same basic mistake - they forget the intended purpose of the task and drift off into their own version of what it should be. Why? Because they don't really understand the need the client wants met or the problem they want solved.

If only they'd SWOT for the test, then they would know which tasks to allocate to which person in the team and how best to communicate with them so they know what to do when. Screw-ups happen when people don't really understand the importance of what's required and they underestimate what's really needed because they are overconfident.

Personally I undertake a SWOT analysis of myself every year, in each sphere of life that I am actively involved in. [Life can be split into seven key spheres. I'll tell you more about them later.] I strongly advise you to do the same. Starting now!

If only someone had thought to do one of these it might have prevented...

The Famous Fleetwood Fox Fiasco

Remember the infamous 1989 Brit Awards hosted by Sam Fox and Mick Fleetwood? I caught a clip of this recently and it is still toe-curlingly embarrassing after all these years. Poor old Sam and Mick, they didn't stand a chance and to be fair it wasn't really their fault. Well not all of it anyway. Whatever could go wrong that night did go wrong but that's what happens when you have a drummer and a former page three girl as presenters of a major awards ceremony that's being televised live instead of employing TV professionals. Speaking of which...

...brings us back to the good ladies of QVC again! Think of all the things a presenter on that channel has to do. And we're only talking in front of the camera, never mind off it! Count 'em up as we go...

Hello Viewers!

She has probably two hours on air of live television. That alone is enough to put most people off. She will have several products to showcase during that time, including demonstrations, possibly with the company head beside her. She has to ask them all sorts of leading questions to allow for the highlighting of the product's features and benefits and still hold a natural-sounding conversation. And sound genuinely interested even if she isn't.

She will have to know the running order for the show, read out item numbers and prices from the studio monitor and keep viewers up to date on stock levels. And speaking of viewers, the phone lines may be opened up during the show and she will now have to deal with members of the public as well! Hello Doris from Scunthorpe...

And all the time she's talking to the audience at home she's got the show's director talking to her in her earpiece. She can't put the audience on hold while she listens to what he's saying to her, she just has to keep going and she'll be professional enough that Doris from Scunthorpe on Line One will never know. [It ain't easy talking and listening at the same time - try it.] And when things go wrong, she will have to think on her feet in front of a live audience. So ladies and gentlemen of the selling community, please show your appreciation with a round of applause for the QVC girls!

Think you could do it?

He Says He's An Actor...

Now you may think that all actors are extrovert attention-grabbers who will do anything for a moment in the spotlight. Nothing could be further from the truth. Sometimes I dread telling people that I'm an actor.

Honest. It's true. When people find out that I'm an actor I get one of two predictable responses. The first is to demand that I do funny voices or impressions of so-and-so for them. I call it Performing Seal Syndrome and no matter how attention-seeking you are it can get intensely tedious. Yes I like getting invites to parties too but they stop being fun when everyone expects you to be the free cabaret.

The other response is the dreaded question "What have you been in?"

I don't know why they ask this question but they always do. They've just been introduced to me, they don't know my name or recognise my face. So even if I was to tell them what I have been in they wouldn't know what it was and wouldn't have seen it anyway!

I know of actors who, when asked that selfsame question, just lie. They take great delight in coming up with the most outlandish acting gig that they can think of. Then they test themselves to see if they can convince their inquisitor that they really are hidden beneath layers of latex in the latest blockbuster movie that's playing in the local multiplex. [Actors love to see how far they can go in the convincibility stakes.]

Of course, you would never catch me doing something so inherently unscrupulous, oh no. No matter how tempting the idea may be...

Actors, like sellers, come in all types, and are just like other regular, ordinary people. The difference is that actors do extraordinary things to not only entertain and delight, but inspire too. That's why actors - the really good, successful ones - get paid such a lot of money. Not everybody can do what they do. Can you?

Homework

Your homework for Chapter 5 is to do a SWOT analysis on yourself, concentrating on your selling skills. Pay particular emphasis to your Weaknesses and any Threats that you can identify.

Think how having the skills of an actor like me could help a seller like you to strengthen those weaknesses, eliminate those threats and gain more sales success as a result.

COMING UP IN CHAPTER 5...

We go on Acronym Alert as Bryan not only defines what an ACTOR is, he also shows us the true meaning of ACTING. See you there!

SWOT Analysis

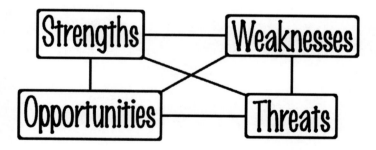

CHAPTER FIVE

ACTORS & ACTING

Before we go on to our first major acronym, I think this is probably as good a place as any to say a word or two about the voluntary emotional torture that is...

The Drama of Drama School

I learned acting by acting. Not many do nowadays. In that period after the Second World War, there were still plenty of places where you could perform in weekly rep and learn by doing. But then, with the advent of television, theatres began to close and nowadays, due to the lack of theatrical opportunities and touring companies, most actors have to go to Drama School to learn their trade, which is a real shame. Don't get me wrong, I have nothing against Drama Schools - and I say that as someone who didn't get in to one - but I remain unconvinced that it can ever be a substitute for an apprenticeship served in a working theatre. Like mine.

That said, there is still a huge amount of snobbery concerning Drama Schools and it puts tremendous pressure on young hopefuls if, like me, they fail to get in. My first audition was for the RSAMD and I've never forgotten the experience. The way these things work is you learn a speech from any Shakespeare play - except that one from Hamlet with the skull - and a speech/monologue from any modern play.

The Audition and its Aftermath

You perform these two pieces for a panel who then ask you what you're going to do if you don't get in, to which the standard answer is, "keep coming back until I do!" Once they've seen everyone they post a list of people who have been given what is termed a Recall, which means they want you to stay for Stage Two. This involves some sort of improvisation where you wake up on a beach, for instance, and find you've been transformed into a fried egg or in a forest where you are a tree whose leaves are about to fall off, really useful stuff like that...

Well, I got a Recall and was overjoyed, only to have my dreams shattered when I got the "Unfortunately, due to the high standard of applicants..." letter a fortnight later. Bar Stewards! Within hours I was in Cumbernauld Theatre Bar getting just as drunk as it was possible to get without you physically retching yourself inside out afterwards.

You don't need to go to Drama School, just as you don't need to go to University. But in the modern profession, it certainly helps. [A fellow actor once told me I should have been born in 1866 instead of 1966 and I knew exactly what he meant by it. The old Actor-Manager! Sometimes I think he was right...]

On the other Hand...

That's not to say that you can't be an actor without Drama School, of course you can. But be prepared to travel a path littered with obstacles that your Drama School Graduate competitors will seldom encounter.

If, as a result of what you've read so far, you feel compelled to have a go at this acting lark then best of luck. But be warned, there's a world of difference between overcoming your nerves and making a Best Man's speech at a friend's wedding, or having enough bottle to belt out your favourite tune at the local Karaoke and being able to get, hold and keep an audience's attention six nights a week, every week, for several months.

Ok, I promised you our first major acronyms in this chapter and so here's something they won't teach you in Drama School:

What Is An ACTOR?

OK, so maybe it's a bit of a predictable choice for an acronym in a book about acting and selling, but hey it works. And we're still in Act One, wait until you see the acronym for SELLING in Act Two!

Anyway, here it is, my very own ACTOR acronym:

A - ACTION

C - CREATION

T - TENSION

O - OBSERVATION

R - REACTION

Good, isn't it! Remember, you saw it here first.

Ok, so let's look at each individual letter in a bit more detail:

A IS FOR ACTION
Action is an audience seeing you doing stuff. Otherwise it's radio.

C IS FOR CREATION
Which is what you do with a character - how he walks and talks etc.

T IS FOR TENSION
Not much drama without it. They say that the essence of all drama is conflict but that doesn't start with a T!

O IS FOR OBSERVATION
Watch real people, see how they behave doing real things and use what you see them do.

R IS FOR REACTION
What you do when other actors speak or do something.

As a seller, you are - or should be - doing these things already. You should be aware of the Tension in a selling scenario, between you and your prospect, a tension that's only released by the decision to buy or not to buy. You Observe your prospect and React accordingly to maintain that connection between the need they want met and your product. You take certain Actions with the intention of Creating an atmosphere where it's easy for your prospect to say yes and become a customer.

Acting and selling aren't that dissimilar, but very few people make the connection. Which is why, as a result of buying this book, you now have an advantage over the competition!

So following on from our definition of an ACTOR, I reckon we should just go the whole hog and do the other one as well, yeah? OK, stand by for the answer to the question:

What is ACTING?

OK, two definitions for this one. The first is:

Actions Characters Take when InteractiNG.

Which is accurate, if not exactly very stylish. So here's the second, in the style of its predecessor:

A - ACTION

C - CREATION

T - TENSION

I - INVESTIGATION

N - NEGATION

G - GENERATION

A IS FOR ACTION
Action is an audience seeing you doing stuff. Otherwise it's radio.

C IS FOR CREATION
Which is what you do with a character - how he walks and talks etc.

T IS FOR TENSION
Not much drama without it. They say that the essence of all drama is conflict but that doesn't start with a "T"!

I IS FOR INVESTIGATION
Getting to know your character as well as you know yourself.

N IS FOR NEGATION
Eliminating anything that undermines the realism of your performance.

G IS FOR GENERATION
Making that all-important connection with the audience.

I'm sure there are lots of other words you could use for each letter. Hmm, I feel another book coming on...

Emotional Availability

Acting requires you to appear to be sad when you're happy, happy when you're sad, angry with people you like and to like people you really can't stand. Whatever the emotional requirements of a scene, you have to be able to portray them convincingly on a nightly basis or at the drop of a hat. So actors have to be what we call 'emotionally available'.

Remember Stan The Man from way back in chapter 2? This is exactly the kind of thing old Stan was on about [which sort of explains why so many actors can be right old drama queens] and as a seller you need to be able to tune into your prospect's emotional wavelength and signal to them that you're right there too.

That's not deception or manipulation that's creating a:

Fictional Reality

It might sound like a contradiction, but every story that is acted out for your entertainment in the movies or on TV - is a created version of the real world. The reason Science Fiction is so appealing to many is simply because it portrays a fictional universe that is far more engaging, entertaining and preferable to the one in which its audience lives. Escapism of the kind we see in the movies or on TV is like a pressure release valve for the stresses and strains of modern life. Yes it can tip over into obsession but if it keeps them off the streets...

A Realistic Unreality

Acting is all about creating another world that can look and sound like the real world but isn't. The fictional reality of a movie or a play needs its own internal cohesion to sustain the scrutiny of an audience. Just as a customer 'buys in' to you and your product, so an audience 'buys in' to what an actor portrays to them.

Each and every story - or ongoing serial narrative - needs its own rules of reality, which must be consistently applied to maintain the loyalty and continued viewing of its audience. One of the problems with this concept is that, as it continues, the audience builds up expectations and it can be a dangerous thing to subvert them or undermine them. Once it stops feeling 'real' to the audience, you've lost them. This is what's meant by 'jumping the shark' and when a show does it, there's no turning back. The unreality of a fictional reality must still be realistic.

Talking To Tolkien

You know that parlour game where you can invite any three famous people - alive, dead or even fictional - to dinner? One of my guests would undoubtedly be JRR Tolkien, author of *The Hobbit* and *The Lord Of The Rings*. [I liked the movie so much I bought the book!] Tolkien talked about what he termed the process of SubCreation, that is, writing something that, although fictional, is so internally consistent that it feels real. His genius in writing LOTR is such that there would arguably be no fantasy genre without him. Good old JRR!

Actors As Sellers

An actor need to know his character as well as a seller knows his product, as well as Tolkien knew his SubCreated world. An actor needs to negate anything that undermines the realism of his performance just as a seller has to overcome any objections a prospect may raise. And finally, an actor has to generate a connection with an audience just as a seller needs to build and maintain rapport with his customers. Are you becoming more aware now of just how linked acting and selling are?

Homework

If you did your homework from chapter 4, you should have a picture of your own strengths and weaknesses. Now I want you to do two more SWOT analyses, one on an actor and one on a seller. See how many parallels you can come up with.

COMING UP IN CHAPTER 6...

Bryan takes us on a guided tour through what, for most folks, is their only personal experience of acting - Amateur Dramatics!

Bryan McCormack

CHAPTER SIX

MAKING A CRISIS OUT OF A DRAMA

If people have done any kind of performing in their life it will probably have been as part of the local Amateur Dramatics Society [in the profession we disparagingly refer to it as AmDram]. Despite its somewhat dodgy reputation, if you've ever been involved in it, then you'll know firsthand a little bit of what the life of an actor is like. That said, there is a world of difference between rehearsing once a week for a three-nights-at-most gig in the local church hall and trying to earn a half-decent living from it.

So you wanna be an Actor, huh?

So let's imagine that you're up for a spot of the old acting with the local AmDram club. Great. First of all, you have to get through the endurance test known as an audition and succeed in getting cast in a role. This usually means picking an audition piece and performing it for the sage Artistic Director who will sit in judgement on your ability. There's an art to this sort of thing on its own and there's a lot more to it than you just working out how to say whatever it is you've chosen. Oh, and realise that you'll have to learn it too, off by heart. [The only actors who read at auditions are the ones that are odds-on to get the part anyway.]

51

That said, sometimes everyone will be given the script and asked which parts they want to try out for. Now this casting method can create all sorts of tensions and rivalries depending on who gets what, so beware. On the plus side though it does prepare you for possible future Golden Envelope Moments, as you wait in anticipation of the Director's announcement of who's got what part.

Getting In The Cast

Assuming it all goes well and you don't get consigned to the ranks of 'Stage Management' you will race home, elated and excited by your great triumph - in which your partner will never seem interested enough - until you actually read the play all the way through and find out what it is they actually expect you to do. It can be a bit of a shocker when you actually find out you're not actually playing the Romantic Lead but actually you're his Bumbling Sidekick, that you're only actually in Act Two and actually you've got hardly any lines. As time goes by however, you may come to realise that - actually - this is a blessing in disguise! Why? Well I can tell you from experience that the best part to play is not always the biggest part you can play...

Learning Your Lines

So now you know who you're playing, what they do in the play and, most important of all for your ego, how many lines they've got. You're going to have to learn all of them too and if you're in a company that aspires to

Non-Professional instead of just Amateur status, there will be no prompt sitting in the wings ready to get you out of a hole with a face-saving whisper if you forget your lines!

The Read-Through

The play will probably be a drama of some sort but if your director is feeling particularly brave you may find yourself in a comedy, in which case it's best to start panicking straight away and get it over with! Then there's the read-through, the first time all the cast are together. All of human life will be here, except that they all have an opinion of their own ability that is often inversely proportional to the amount of talent that they actually have... this will be of great benefit to you as you become aware of both the hierarchy and pecking order in the group.

As you might expect, at a read-through you read through the entire play, including stage directions, to get an idea of what it's actually going to be like and how long it'll last. This can be quite nerve-wracking as it's here that you suddenly realise just what it is you've let yourself in for! Then there's the question of how you want to play the part you've been given versus how the director wants you to play the part he's given you!

Who Am I Playing Again?

There are all sorts of questions about this character that you will have to find answers to. How old is he? Where does he come from? What does he do? What does he look like? What is he after? Is he a Hero or a Villain? [The latter are always the more fun to play.] The text of the play should give you clues to or tell you clearly about most of this. [Anything that's not explicit or implied in the text that you make up yourself is what we call 'back-story'.] Does he have to kiss anyone? [Can be tricky if you have to put a lip lock on someone's wife. Like the director's for instance. And if your Leading Lady's husband just happens to be a black-belt bodybuilder...]

And quite apart from all that - how does he speak? This last one can sometimes be obvious from the structure of the dialogue but you'll still have to work out how you are going to say the lines and determine whether or not to use an accent. You will usually find that the inability to do an accent convincingly will not stop your more 'experienced' colleagues from using one anyway...

Rehearsals

Remember too that you will have to keep whatever night of the week it is you're rehearsing free, every week, for however many weeks it is until Opening Night. Then there's the question of what you're going to wear and how you're going to look in it [always important, that one]. Next there's the tricky business of learning your moves or blocking as it's known, which means where you are on the stage when you say what you say and do what you do.

You'll also have to negotiate the minefield that is props - guns that don't fire, doors that won't open, that kind of thing. Not to mention the fact that you'll be sharing the stage most of the time with other AmDrammers who will probably forget their lines or their cues. Cues are reminders for actors, telling them they need to Do Something Important when they hear it - like come onstage when they're supposed to, that kind of thing!

The week of the show, and depending on its complexity, there will be a Technical Rehearsal to contend with. This is simply where you top and tail each scene and rehearse all the lighting and scenery changes as well as any sound effects and pyrotechnics [if your director is particularly sadistic]. Actors have been known to crash into the scenery in the dark and it helps if everyone knows who's off where and who's on when.

Dress Rehearsal

The Dress Rehearsal is everybody's last chance to practice before an unsuspecting audience is herded into the church hall to endure - sorry, enjoy, the fruits of your collective labours. In essence it's a show without an audience and is played as if there really was a paying audience in that empty theatre. If something goes wrong, you need to find a way out of it. It can also be your last chance to iron out any technical problems that may have been plaguing the production. Tomorrow night when you walk onstage it will be in front of real people who have paid good money to watch you, so it had better be good. No pressure there, then!

And just because you're in an AmDram company, don't think an audience's expectations are any lower. Neither should you think that they want you to fail. Yes, you can get unexpected laughs when things go wrong but that can work in your favour. They want you to succeed, unless they're the Stage Manager that really wanted to play your part...

Showtime!

Opening Night is as bad as it gets, believe me. After that it's not exactly plain sailing but you've already done it once and survived so tomorrow will be a lot easier and you can start to relax a bit and enjoy it. Until that is something unexpected goes wrong. Think about what you would do if someone falls ill - very few AmDram groups can afford the luxury of understudies. So by way of illustration of the kind of thing you can expect to encounter, here is a personal example...

The play was called, *The Death & Life Of Sneaky Fitch* and I played the Reverend Stanley Blackwood. It was a comedy western and I adopted a chicken walk and my best Boston accent for the part [I was 16 at the time, gimme a break!]. As is the norm, it was a three nighter - Thursday to Saturday. The Wednesday was the Dress Rehearsal [some shows have been known to have more than one] and the Tuesday was the Tech Run.

Thursday was a good opener and Friday saw the obligatory saloon gal character played by girl #2 instead of girl #1 because girl #1 couldn't do Friday for some reason but would be back on Saturday! So last night of a three-night run that we've been working on for months comes around and the director asks for a word with me before curtain up. Apparently they're having a fund-raising raffle in the interval and could I host it? Well of course I could but it'd mean missing out on the interval break that the rest of the cast would be enjoying. He then assured me that he could set me up with girl #1 at the after-show party so...

I hosted the raffle in the interval but here's the twist - I did it entirely in character! It felt wrong to come out of character in the interval when we still had the second half to do, so the Rev Stanley Blackwood did the raffle instead of Bryan, ably assisted by a few members of the audience. The whole thing was a great success and probably the highlight of the evening for some. But the best bit was after the show was over when an American couple asked me what part of the States I was from! And before you make any smartarse remarks about their gullibility, I like to think it was the quality of my entirely ad-libbed performance...

Still wanna be an Actor?

Obviously the only reason they asked me to do the raffle - with one hour's notice, I might add - was because they knew I could handle it. But I don't think anyone expected me to do it in character! You need to be prepared for anything in this game and if none of that has managed to put you off, or even worse, inspired you to have a go, then good luck to you. Believe me, you will need it. Oh, and one final thing, if ever you are unfortunate enough to find yourself doing a musical or even worse, a pantomime, then you have my both deepest sympathy and the urgent recommendation that you seek medical assistance as soon as possible…

But before you start to criticise me for being a bit harsh on the old AmDrammers, then please realise that everything I've just said applies equally well to the world of professional theatre. And in case you are still wondering what this has to do with selling, think back for a moment and see how many similarities you can spot between the two worlds. There are plenty of them, I can assure you. As we shall see later, the twin worlds of both the professional actor and the professional seller have more in common then you might think. It's just that acting's better - I mean, when did you last get a round of applause for making a sale? And I don't mean the staff, I'm talking about the customers!

So for all the frustration, tantrums, petty jealousy, sexual tension and sphincter-releasing, sheer nerve-shredding terror of anticipation as you wait in the wings - about to possibly make a complete fool of yourself in front of your friends and family, assuming you have any left who will admit to knowing you by the end of the show - when you finally get out there and get your first laugh, when you realise that, despite your doubts, you really do have a talent for this sort of thing, then in the words of - yes, that song - there really is no feeling quite like it. And anticipating your next question yes, that does include sex.

COMING UP IN CHAPTER 7...

We start to get serious about acting and selling as Bryan shares with us his first Big Secret and starts to reveal the real truth about acting.

See you there!

Bryan McCormack

CHAPTER SEVEN

THE TRUTH ABOUT ACTING! (PART ONE)

The fact is that acting is not just a highly competitive industry but one that is overmanned and under-resourced, with too many actors chasing too few jobs from too few employers.

Of course, there's nothing to stop the enterprising actor going out there, writing his own hit show and getting noticed as a result. It's called the Edinburgh Fringe and it can be both a springboard and a graveyard.

But what many hopefuls arriving at Edinburgh Waverley from London Euston fail to recognise is The Real Secret To Getting Ahead In Acting. Those who have realised this secret, and applied it effectively, are the ones that you are seeing on television and in the movies today. They realised early on that those who enter the acting profession do not compete on equal terms. And I don't mean having a famous actor for a father or being a RADA graduate.

Ladies and Gentlemen, Boys and Girls, Stand By for:

The First Big Secret

When I first started out as an actor, I was naïve enough to think that I would turn up at an audition and that my considerable talent would be so obvious that of course I would get the part. Needless to say, after the first few auditions where I didn't get the part I had to rethink my view - and fast. It was obvious that I had got it seriously wrong. The profession didn't work the way I thought it did. I had to change my approach - and fast - and find out how the acting world really worked. And what do you think it was that I discovered?

Talent, by itself, is not enough.

I'll say that again. Talent, by itself, is not enough for success as an actor. Or a seller, come to that. In fact in any area of life it holds true. This is the key foundation for everything else I'm going to teach you so here it is once more:

Talent, by itself, is not enough.

Talent + What? = Success

In this book we're talking about two worlds, acting and selling, and how having an understanding of the one can help you succeed in the other. In both these worlds, or any other you can think of, talent by itself is never enough for real success because for that to happen you need two other things. Before we come to them though let's be clear on what we think talent is.

What Is Talent?

The simplest definition that I could come up with for talent is:

THE NATURAL ABILITY TO DO SOMETHING WELL

Imagine a cross-country runner starting five minutes later than everybody else, but still finishing the race first. That's what talent will do for you.

I have always had a talent for acting and performing. As I said earlier I started at primary school by reciting poetry at the age of eight. The poetry in question was by Robert Burns and the competition I won required me to repeat my performance for the local Burns Club.

When I got my first laugh I realised something had been released in me and eventually, after all those school plays, all those songs with the choir [Tenor Soloist until my voice broke to bass baritone with just a touch of falsetto, thanks for asking], all those AmDram Clubs, that stint in Hospital Radio, Youth Theatre, the Drama School disappointments, my first One-Man-Show [ten days before my 18th birthday!], five years volunteer work as unpaid assistant to Bill Winter...

...it's November 1987 and - tadah! - "I say Bryan, old boy, equity card up for grabs as acting assistant stage manager on the old panto this year, how d'you fancy it, joining the jolly theatre company, what?" And that's how I became an actor! [And before you ask, no Robert Robson did not speak like that, that was just for comic effect.]

At school my best subject was always English - as you can probably tell - but my worst subject? Sport. I was one of the legion of sensitive kids or 'poofters' as we were known back in the 1970s. I was rubbish at sport and dreaded PE lessons. Football? Two left feet. Rugby? Oh no. My survival instinct was far too healthy to let me get involved in that one.

The only sport I was halfway decent at was running. So I was always able to make a quick getaway. Handy thing to have, that...

A Bit More About Talent

Ok, let's talk a bit more about this talent malarkey - please note the following important differences:

> TALENT is something that you Have whereas an
>
> ABILITY is something that you Learn and a
>
> SKILL is something you Develop

The Dictionary definitions of talent, ability and skill may be similar but they are different. Essentially this means there are:

Three Kinds Of Sellers

You can either have:

> A TALENT FOR SELLING

or you can have

> THE ABILITY TO SELL

or you can be

> SKILLED AT SELLING

Which one best describes you? The vast majority of the sellers I have come across fall into the second category. To really make significant progress, you have to get yourself into that all-important third category.

And you will, because remember, we agreed to work together to make you The Best Seller You Can Be, didn't we? See, I hadn't forgotten!

In exactly the same way as sellers like you, people in my profession of acting can have:

A TALENT FOR ACTING

or they can have

THE ABILITY TO ACT

or they can be

SKILLED AT ACTING

And if you're me then you can do both! And then you write a book…

Solving The Prosperity Puzzle

Whatever our individual talents are, certain things always hold true in every case. As follows:

Your talent, whatever it is, should, above all, be:

PRACTICAL

By that I mean it does/has three things:

1. It meets a NEED

2. It solves a PROBLEM and

3. There is a MARKET for it.

All fairly obvious stuff. But there's more. Your talent should also be:

PERSONAL - It's WHO you are

PROFITABLE - It gets RESULTS for you

PLEASURABLE - It SATISFIES you

PURPOSEFUL - It's WHY you are Who You Are!

Homework

What talents and abilities do you have? List them all, paying attention to the five Ps. These are your future, your potential revenue streams, your means of achieving your goals and dreams. Once you've done that, go back and look at your SWOT analysis and compare the two. If you can find any areas of convergence, congratulations - you've just found out what you're meant to do with your life!

COMING UP IN CHAPTER 8...

We delve deeper into the notion that talent alone is not enough as Bryan reveals the two other things you need for real success. See you there!

CHAPTER EIGHT

THE TRUTH ABOUT ACTING (PART TWO)

So, to recap, talent is "a natural ability to do something well" but by itself, that's not enough for success. When I look back I can think of several really talented people that I used to work with - and I have no idea where they are today.

Where Are They Now?

For instance, of all the people I worked with back in my Youth Theatre days, I only know of one guy who's achieved any modicum of success - as a regular on a soap. He was one of four of us who all auditioned for the RSAMD the same year. The other three got in, I didn't. So where are the other two? Maybe they're both raking it in and having a whale of a time on the cruise ships. But I doubt it.

How many people from your own life can you look back on and say that, out of all of us they were most likely to succeed but when I look around today I have to ask where are they now?

If talent alone was enough to guarantee success, you and I would be up there with all those Hollywood A-Listers by now, if not taking their place. But it's not enough. And they know that. But don't worry, soon enough, you'll know it too.

So what's missing? Ok, I'll tell you. But before I do, I want to remind you of something very important and it's this:

The Triangle of Fire

Ever been subjected to one of those hellish 1980s Health and Safety films with porno-esque synth music and acting that would make even the worst AmDrammer cringe? Me too. The only thing I can clearly recall is The Fire Triangle. I mention it because that principle of triangulation applies equally well to the world of acting. And selling too, come to that.

So what are the three things you need if you're going to start a fire?

OXYGEN, HEAT & FUEL

If any one of these three elements is missing, you don't have a fire! You need to combine all three before you can commence your combustion. Like so:

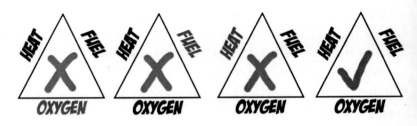

So applying this same principle to acting and selling, of the three elements we need for our triangle we so far only have one - talent.

What are the other two that we're missing? And what are we going to call this triangle anyway? How's about:

The Triangle of Triumph

Sounds a bit more snazzy than The Success Triangle, don't ya think? Well, I do and it's my book so Triangle of Triumph it is! And anyway, a triumph is better than a success - it's an outstanding success! Don't you want to be known as an outstanding success at selling? I mean, you do still want to be The Best Seller You Can Be, right? Just checking.

Now, just like The Triangle of Fire, our Triangle of Triumph needs a combination of three things before we can get a result, thus:

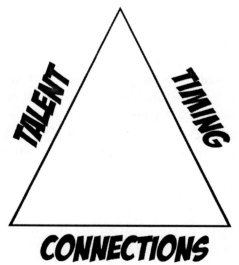

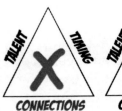

Talent, Timing & Connections

Let's define those three things before we go any further.

TALENT

Talent is the natural ability to do something well. So on those terms...

Acting talent is the natural ability to perform; to engage, entertain and convince an audience. You don't have to work at it or learn it, somehow you can just do it straightaway. And that immediately puts you ahead of the competition.

But what about timing?

TIMING

There is much more to timing than simply being in the right place at the right time. We often talk about comedians who have a great sense of timing. Comic timing, for both actors and stand-ups is a matter of knowing exactly the right moment to say your punch line. Leave the pause just that bit too long or leave too short a gap and you diminish the impact it has. Remember an audience can only laugh when they're not listening to the dialogue.

Getting your timing right can mean the difference between moving your career to the next level and heading down a dead end. Just remember this: The clock of your life is constantly ticking and you only get one shot at it before the alarm goes off. Timing is not just a case of being in the right place at the right time or you will never make it - Timing is the capacity to discern the moment of maximum impact.

And lastly, what about connections?

CONNECTIONS

Connections are usually defined as something that links two people or things together. We talk about making contacts or being connected to someone. You meet someone who introduces you to someone they know that you don't. But now you do. But not only do you know them, they know you. This new contact has contacts of his own that you are now connected to via him. The more people you are connected to, the more potential sources of problem solving you have access to. This handy diagram illustrates what I mean.

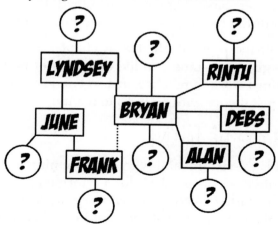

I know Rintu - The Very Nice Man who wrote the Foreword - and we have a mutual friend in Alan. But Rintu does not know my friend Lyndsey. I know Lyndsey's friend June by sight only but June knows Frank and I knew Frank years ago. Potentially I am connected to everyone that everyone that I am connected to is connected to too!

As a seller, I am sure you can see the potential for sales in this principle.

When Floyd Met Lloyd...

Some people say it's not what you know it's who you know. I disagree. I think it's not who you know, it's who knows you! Seriously, who do you know that can open doors for you? Who do you know who lunches at The Ivy? Look at the late Keith Floyd, his TV career took off because his producer ate in his restaurant and thought, "this bloke would be great on the telly". It would never have happened if Lloyd didn't know Floyd. It didn't happen because Floyd knew Lloyd!

We'll talk more about all this in chapter 9 but first I want to give you some real-life examples of how these three things work in practice, just so you know that this isn't all just theory with no basis in reality!

An example of TALENT

If talent is the natural ability to do something well, then I have always had a talent for performing. As I said earlier, I started aged 8 by winning a Burns poetry recitation competition that they held in primary school.

I won that competition three times out of five, which isn't bad. I once did a Youth Training Scheme video where I played five different roles, before he was famous I played straight man to Craig Ferguson, I did my first one-man show ten days before my 18th birthday… I could fill this entire book with examples of things my talent has allowed me to do, but that's not what we're here for. Instead, here's an example from my selling career to be going on with - the first call centre that I worked in, I was made team captain within the first month. And three months and one week after I started I was made a team leader. Not bad, eh?

An example of TIMING

Timing is the capacity to discern the moment of maximum impact. Here's a story of how someone got their timing just right. This story involves four people - me, Andy, Lynn and Marie. We all worked at the same place at one time but one by one we all moved on. Lynn first, then me, then Andy and finally Marie. So I'm out this one day and bump into Andy. We start playing catch-up and asking where we are now. Seems Andy was in town and popped in to see Lynn, who told him that Marie was now working in a shop just down the road. So Andy pops down to see Marie who tells him that her boss is looking for someone. Andy pops over to see her boss and gets the job! Timing, see? [Fact - more than 50% of all jobs are not advertised!]

An example of CONNECTIONS

The story of how this book came to be is a great example of the power of connections. Just in case you missed it earlier, I'm a great fan of Doctor Who. And I was a fan back in the days when it certainly wasn't as cool to be a fan as it is now! I joined the Glasgow Who group in January 2009, where I met Rintu and Alan. Now Alan had run the group single-handedly for the previous five years and had understandably had enough. Just after the group's Army of Guests Convention at the end of May, I was asked to be Meetings Co-ordinator. This meant I took charge of the monthly pub meetings, something I was more than happy to do. As a result of that, Alan asked me to do one of the interview slots at the next event. It was after seeing me at the event that Rintu suggested I write this book that you are reading now.

So if Rintu hadn't suggested it, you probably wouldn't be reading this book. Rintu probably wouldn't have suggested it if he hadn't seen me interviewing and I wouldn't have met Rintu if I hadn't joined the group!

But I've got an even better example than that which illustrates all three!

Bryan's Ultimate Example

This is the true story of how I got my Equity Card and my Agent.

I started with Cumbernauld Youth Theatre in January 1983. John Haswell was the Director and one day he asked if anyone was willing to volunteer to help the Stage Manager with some clearing out that needed doing. Well my hand was up in the air straight away and that was the start of a five year unpaid apprenticeship to Bill Winter. There was too much work for Bill and his assistant but not enough for three - really it was a two and a half man job and I was the half!

After the opening night of the Adult Drama Group's production "Gryme Eagle" [which we immediately christened "Durty Budgie"!] I was sat in the bar when Robert Robson, the theatre's Artistic Director asked if he could have a word. He took me to one side and said that the panto was coming up soon and there was a Card going for an Acting Assistant Stage Manager. Did I want it? Bit of a daft question really. Of course it turns out that everyone knew about this except me and Bill Winter still says it the only time he's ever known me to be lost for words!

And so, having recovered from the initial shock, it's on to rehearsals for my first ever professional performance with Cumbernauld Theatre Company. The panto was "A Christmas Carol". I played The Boy Is Ignorance [no lines to learn!], a carol singer, one of Fezziwig's guests and the boy who gets sent for the turkey. I was also responsible for helping set the stage between shows, making sure all props were in position and more importantly, I understudied both the actor who played Scrooge - whose name I forget, apologies! - and a contemporary of mine called Neil McKinven, who was the only one of the lot of us to go to RADA. Neil played Scrooge's Nephew, Marley's Ghost and The Ghost of Christmas Present.

Now being an understudy means you have to learn that actor's roles as well as your own and if he falls ill, then you have to go 'on' instead. Well, during any long run - and especially panto - it's inevitable that someone will get the lurgy at least once. And so it was that one day, after the morning performance that Bill Winter comes to me and says Neil's ill and I'm on. So it's lunchtime, the next show is in an hour, you can just imagine the scene. We are now frantically trying to rearrange the entire show to take account of Neil's absence. The first thing is to sit down and work out which of my own roles I can still do and which, logistically, I just can't [For instance, I can hardly be The Boy Is Ignorance and The Ghost of Xmas Present at the same time!] and then it's a case of the rubber hitting the road and seeing if I really have remembered Neil's lines as well as my own!

Well we did the matinee and I've never sweated so much in all my life. In fact I remember being utterly exhausted by the whole experience but exhilarated by the prospect of having to do it all again that night! And so come the evening performance, I'm once again playing half a dozen roles. And in the audience that night is, guess who? Pat Lovett, the woman who would become my agent. That night was the only night she was in to see the show and if I hadn't been 'on' for Neil, it's much less likely that she would have taken me on, as there would have been a lot less for her to see!

How many examples of talent, timing and connections did you see at work in that story? How many examples can you think of from your own life where all three of these have been at work?

Homework

Take a few moments to map out your own connections in the same way that I did earlier in this chapter. Sit down with a nice hot cuppa and a blank sheet of paper and draw a circle in the centre of the page with your name in it. Now think of all the people you know and add them to the map. Start with friends and family, then people at work and work your way through all the different areas of your life. Check your mobile or an old address book, you'll be amazed at not only how many people you are, or have been, connected to and just how many you've lost touch with. Maybe after completing this exercise you should give them a call…

COMING UP IN CHAPTER 9...

We learn more about how your talent, timing and connections can all add up to Success. See you there!

Bryan McCormack

CHAPTER NINE

THE TRUTH ABOUT ACTING (PART THREE)

In the previous chapter I introduced you to the three success elements that you need to combine together if you are going to make a success of your life, in either acting or selling:

TALENT

Acting Talent is the natural ability to perform; to engage, entertain and convince an audience.

TIMING

Timing is the capacity to discern the moment of maximum impact.

CONNECTIONS

Connections are not just contacts, they are customers for your talent.

In order to attain success - at anything, not just acting or selling - you must have talent, timing and connections. All three together. I call this:

The TTC Principle

...and, since I've discerned it, I've seen it at work time and again. Now that you are beginning to understand how it works, you'll start to see it too.

For instance, if you have an amazing talent for sales, but can't earn a living from it, what good is it? [Talent should be practical, remember?] That's Talent without Timing or Connections.

Or, if you have an amazing talent for sales and you know someone in the firm you want to work for but they have just filled all their vacancies, you've got Talent and Connections but lousy Timing.

Or if you've got an amazing talent for sales and you get your application in on time but you have no champion within the company, then you've got Talent and Timing with no Connections.

Think back for a moment over your own life. Count up how many times you missed out because one of these three essential success elements was missing. Count how many times you could have applied this principle and then think about where you could be today if only you had known this principle that I've just shared with you. You see, I told you you'd be glad you invested in this book!

But if you've got your three TTC elements in place, what do you get?

They are not an end in themselves and attaining all three is not the guarantee of success you may think it is. When they combine, when you get convergence, you get something else that is vital for progress any success in any career, not just selling.

Before we get to that, let's go over what I mean by:

Convergence

Convergence is when the separate elements of success come together in just the right way at just the right time.

Convergence is when all the individual elements that make up the mix are all present in the correct proportions. Convergence is an open door that leads to your purpose, your calling, your destiny if you like. Life is much better when you believe there is a purpose for having it.

Convergence is the gateway to doing what you are meant to do, being who you are meant to be. Sadly, the evidence is that very few people believe they have attained convergence in their lives, that they have fulfilled the dreams of their youth.

Too many of us though get the exact opposite in our lives - divergence, a mismatch of these success elements.

I can certainly think back to times in my life when I made decisions that took me off the path that I wanted my life to follow and it's taken me years to finally get it back on track [this book is part of that process]. Think back on your own life and I'm sure you can come up with several such instances of your own.

Divergence is a deviation from the path that leads to fulfilling your dreams, doing what you really want to do, being who you want to be and having a trunk full of great memories to look back on.

So what is the single most vital thing that having loads of Talent, a great sense of Timing and helpful

Connections gives you? Think about it, how can simply having all three of these things advance your career and get you closer to your purpose? They must combine together to produce something else that provides a vehicle for your talent, something that enables it to develop, helps it grow and reach a wider audience.

Can you guess what that is?

In this diagram, the lines from each of the three points of the triangle are the lines of convergence, meeting at the swirly thing in the middle. But what is it? What does the swirly thing represent?

TALENT + TIMING + CONNECTIONS = ?

Here's a clue - think of the swirly thing as a portal, a doorway if you like, into the future. An opening into what you are not doing yet, something that someone has to give you, something you need before you can move to that next level. [That last one should really have given it away.] Have you worked it out yet?

OPPORTUNITIES, that's what you get!

When your Talent makes a Connection at the right Time, when you get convergence, then you get an Opportunity.

You can have all the Talent in the world but if your Timing is off, you will never be in the right place at the right time to make a Connection and grab an Opportunity.

If you're in the wrong place at the right time, or the right place at the wrong time, there won't be an Opportunity for your Talent to shine.

$$T + T + C = O$$

If you don't make Connections, then they won't get you to the next place you need to be. If you miss the last bus of Opportunity, then you'll need to walk - you'll still get there in the end, but it'll take a heck of a lot longer than it needed to. And there's no guarantee anybody will still be there when you finally arrive!

Opportunity

An Opportunity is a temporary time of optimum advantage due to favourable conditions.

You've heard the phrase "window of opportunity" I'm sure. That's because there's only a short timeframe within which you can take advantage of that favourable conjunction of circumstances. It's a bit like an eclipse - it only happens when everything is in perfect alignment, and that doesn't last forever.

So Opportunities, when taken, give you an advantage. But what's an advantage?

Advantage

An advantage is a unique attribute capable of advancing your talent.

By definition, an advantage is something you have that your opponent doesn't have. So let's put all this together, shall we?

TTC - The Formula for Success

1. You must have the three essential components of TTC:
    * Talent - the natural ability to do something well
    * Timing - the capacity to discern the moment of maximum impact
    * Connections - customers for your talent

2. Opportunities arise when you get those three elements in Convergence
    *   an Opportunity is a temporary time of optimum advantage

3. An Advantage is a unique attribute capable of advancing your talent

SUCCESS CHECKLIST

TALENT ☐

TIMING ☐

CONNECTIONS ☐

OPPORTUNITIES ☐

ADVANTAGES ☐

Once you have gained that advantage - a promotion, say - then the process begins all over again at this new level. I've illustrated it as a triangle but you could just as easily picture it another way - a Venn Diagram of three intersecting circles for instance or a door with three locks that won't open without all three keys [we'll talk about how to harness the power of your imagination in a later chapter].

COMING UP IN CHAPTER 10...

We finally learn what it is about actors that sellers need to know as Bryan gives us the low-down on what actors are really all about.

See you there!

CHAPTER TEN

THE TRUTH ABOUT ACTORS!

Actors are unique amongst sales people in that they only ever sell one product. A product that is bespoke and individually tailored to the actor's marketplace. As a seller, you sell one of three things:

1. Your client's product
2. Your employer's product
3. Your own product

Actors fall into the third category but in a unique way.

Acting is Selling

As we've seen, talent is no guarantee of success. That applies to selling just as much as it does to acting, or indeed any area of life. Often the politician totally lacking in charisma can still get elected. Some of the greatest musicians will never have a number one hit. That's not to say that you can't find fulfilment without fame, far from it. But if success is judged purely on results, and in sales there's no other yardstick, then being The Best and recognised as such is the ultimate aim. So if it's not talent that gets you the gold medal of success, then what does? Why is it that the most talented are not always the first to the finishing line?

The answer is that the most successful actors are not those with the most talent, but those who have realised that they are a marketable commodity in a competitive marketplace.

Think about it. As a seller, you know that price is only an issue for your customers when all other things are equal. Take Car Insurance. When you sell Insurance you need to ascertain the level of cover the customer needs. Then, when you get the quote, if the price is higher than their current insurer, you need to do a comparison.

You point out that, whilst their current insurer may be cheaper, their cover doesn't have all the bells and whistles that yours does. We give you this, that and the next thing. You have to justify the extra expense by convincing the customer that the additional benefits are worth the extra outlay. But if the price is the same, and the level of cover is the same, then your challenge is to convince that customer to move their business to you instead. Actors find themselves in the same position at auditions. There may be several hundred people under consideration or a shortlist of a dozen. An actor has to do just what you have to do with your customer - give them a reason to decide in your favour.

The Second Big Secret

As an actor, my speciality is characters and voices. So if I go for an audition, I will stand a better chance if that's what they're looking for. [Remember there are only two kinds of actor - character and personality.] But there are lots of actors who can do funny voices. Why should they pick me instead of someone else? And this is where the real secret lies.

A seller sells a product. Even if it is his own product, it is still an object. An actor is his own product, he is selling himself.

Actors have to sell themselves as a brand, a product. That is why they make better sellers than most sales people.

An actor is his own product.

An actor is many things, but possibly the most important of all the things that he is, and the one thing he must never, ever forget is this:

Remember You're A PRIAM !

This is absolutely vital for your success, whether you're an actor or a seller or both - every single person, you included, is a PRIAM.

What the heck is a PRIAM I hear you ask? My pleasure! A PRIAM is a

PRODUCT RETAILING IN A MARKETPLACE

Whatever your Marketplace is - whatever sphere of life you are looking to be employed in or find success in - you must remember that You [who you are, what you know, who you know, what you can do, what you've done] are a product looking for a customer. Anything that requires an audience or anything that requires a customer is a PRIAM.

So for the remainder of this chapter, here are some observations on the people who populate my chosen profession. As you read, see if you can work out how being a PRIAM applies to each one and to you as a seller.

Why Actors Fail

The reason many hopefuls fail in their acting career is that they forget, or worse still never realise until it's too late, that they are not just a talented individual, they are a product competing against hundreds of similar products that all do the same basic job. I didn't realise that when I first started out, though in my defence nobody, including my Agent, told me. Perhaps they just assumed I already knew…

Don't Tell Me - Show Me!

Remember that scene in *My Fair Lady* where Eliza sings to Freddie, "Don't talk about love - show me!"? Well, in exactly the same way, an actor needs to demonstrate his talent, not just talk about it. An actor needs to take every opportunity he can get his hands on to show how talented and versatile [i.e. employable] he is.

As an actor you are always 'on' as we say and aware that everyone you meet is a potential connection [and what are connections again…?]

And don't forget Hyperboy and Hypergirl - if you're making yourself out to be something you're not, you will get found out eventually.

The Spotlight. Getting in it is one thing...

... but staying in it is quite another. You need to remember that the reason many actors are insecure is because they know that potentially each new job they get could also be their last. [Just like each sale a seller gets could be his last for a long time too.] The Spotlight of public attention and affection is constantly on the move, like The Eye of Sauron, always looking for something different, something new.

There is always the danger that, as a product in the entertainment marketplace, you will reach the end of your Shelf Life before you are ready to stickered down to half price and thrown in the Reduced To Clear section. That's why I find voice work so rewarding. There's none of the attendant hassle that goes with complete strangers knowing what you look like. And you get to have a longer career too!

Crossing The ARID Desert

Ever seen the WW2 movie, "Ice Cold In Alex"? Harry Andrews, Sylvia Sim, Anthony Quayle and John Whatsisname, trekking though the desert in a jeep towards Alexandria, motivated by the thought of an ice cold beer and one of them is a German spy. Brilliant film. Sometimes trying to get a sale can be a bit like trekking through the desert too...

We've all had those barren patches where nothing seems to work, everything that used to work has stopped working and as a result we wander through the wilderness of rejection, searching desperately for an oasis of receptiveness. So here's a little acronym [Oh we do love our acronyms, don't we!] to help you get through those tough times.

Every sale a seller makes and every audition an actor undertakes is a process. And it's the same 4 stage process, whether it's an actor and a director or a seller and a prospect and applies equally to both parties:

1. ACTIONS - the things you do to achieve your goal

2. REACTIONS - the way they respond to what you do

3. INTERACTIONS - the way you communicate your goal

4. DECISIONS - the choices you make based on steps 1-3

The key to getting through the barren no-sales desert is to remember the alternate version of this acronym:

A - ADAPTIVE

R - RESPONSES

I - INITIATE

D - DIFFERENCES

Most sellers and actors fall down on Stage 2. It's not so much the actions you take that cause problems as your reaction to the actions of others that kill the sale. You need to change your reaction to their action as it's the only thing you have any control over [this works for failing relationships as well as for sales…]

The Definition of Madness

...is to carry on doing the same thing but expecting a different result. If the approach you always use, the one that always works, isn't working any more - change your approach! If you keep running into a brick wall, then stop running - if you want to end up with something different, then you need to do something different!

The Essential Difference

Speaking of differences, aside from the obvious fact that one gets paid for pretending to be someone else and the other doesn't, here is the real difference between an amateur actor and a professional actor.

The amateur loves acting and prefers doing it to anything else. The professional lives for acting and hates having to do something else. And the professional knows that he has to sell himself, not just show off how talented he is. There are only really two reasons for becoming an actor - because you love doing it and would rather do it than anything else or because you have to do it and you know in your heart that you just can't do anything else.

Does selling do that to you? Does the prospect of going back out there and having to hit your Sales Target all over again fill you with the same kind of excitement that an actor gets before he goes on stage? If it does, if selling is in your blood like acting is in mine, then I'm very happy for you. But I doubt it.

What It Takes To Be A Winner

It was, I believe, the late Edwin Louis Cole who summed it up best: "Winners are not those who never fail but those who never quit!" Isn't that great? There's nothing wrong with failure, sometimes it can teach us more than our successes. And yes, I'm big enough to admit that I've made more than my fair share of mistakes as both an actor and a seller, some of them real howlers. Looking back now I can see that some of them were avoidable, some were inevitable. If you are going to become The Best Seller You Can Be - if you really want to be a winner in the game of life - then you must learn how to tell them apart. And quickly, there isn't much time left. Oh I know you think you've got all the time in the world but I can assure you, one minute you're 16, the next you're 40 and asking yourself, "Where did the time go?"

Glass, Bottle, Bottle, Glass

The late magician Tommy Cooper used to do a routine where a glass and a bottle would be on a table in front of him. He would place a sleeve over each of them, distract the audience with some gags and when the sleeves were removed they had miraculously swapped places. Thinking of that routine always reminds me of that question, "Is your glass half empty or half full?" For years I used to say half empty but now I prefer to say neither as it's constantly being topped up from the nearby bottle!

In other words, don't give up, it's never too late and real success is not the money you make but the way what you do makes you feel inside. That's what really counts. Keep that in mind, and no matter the external appearance, you will always be a winner to yourself!

COMING UP IN CHAPTER 11...

We learn the secret to marketing yourself as Bryan reveals how to become self-aware instead of self-conscious. See you there!

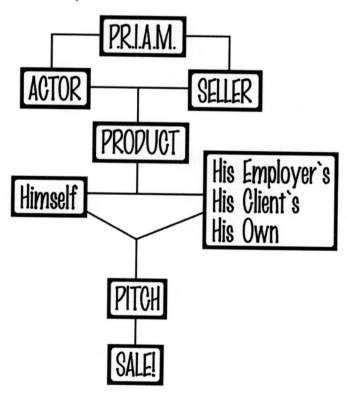

Bryan McCormack

CHAPTER ELEVEN

SELL YOURSELF! TO YOURSELF!

So now we know what the business of acting is really all about. Actors are products and talent counts for much less than you think. If you lack talent but can be marketed effectively you can still make it - you just need to look at any of today's plastic pop stars to see that. An actor must know how to effectively sell himself as a product and needs to have a marketing strategy just like anyone else selling any other product.

The Secret of Real Success

But before we get into that, please realise that it isn't all about a gold star on your Dressing Room door. It isn't about the money or the fame. It isn't about your flash motor or the dolly bird on your arm. Success isn't about awards ceremonies and red carpets or getting your name above the title. All that is just symbolic success. You may have all of the outward trappings, but that doesn't mean you're fulfilled. The history of both entertainment and showbusiness is chock full of people whose personal lives were a complete mess, but to Joe Public everything looked as enviable as ever from the outside looking in.

Real, lasting success comes from inside. Every actor [and seller] must be utterly, completely and totally convinced that they really are good. So what if nobody agrees with you, it's your opinion that counts, not theirs! And why?

Me, Her, Him – You Choose!

If free will isn't just an illusion then it is surely the ability to choose. Every day we make choices based on the information we have at our disposal and our interpretation of what it means. Sometimes everybody has an opinion, but no-one has any advice. But there's one person you can always count on to be there for you, one person you can always rely on to be there when you need someone to help you. And who is it? Why it's YOU of course!

Think about it, you spend more time with you than anyone else. I will only see you for a few hours a day at most, you are with yourself 24/7. [So you see, you're never really alone. It just seems like it...] And the point is that you will believe you before you believe me or anyone else!

Internal Dialogue

That voice in your head, you know the tiny little voice that's always there, in your head, talking to you? That's your voice, that is! We call it internal dialogue or self-talk. You may prefer to use the term 'thoughts' to describe your dialogue with yourself but whatever you call it, it's going on in your head all the time. Including right now.

In your brain there are currently three co-existent states of being. And I'm sure you've got more than enough smarts to know that they are:

YOUR PAST - your remembering of what has happened to you.

YOUR PRESENT - your understanding of what is happening to you.

YOUR POTENTIAL - your imagining of what might happen to you.

[See what I did there? You were expecting the old Past, Present, Future routine weren't you? Ha ha, fooled ya! And, with one chapter to go, that leaves the half-time score at several million to nil, to me!]

I dislike the term 'future' as it always seems to carry the implication that there is something pre-determined and unavoidable about what's coming down the pipe. Sorry, but there is no such thing as luck and fatalism is just the same old victim mentality with a different self-pitying mask on.

You have a potential out there waiting for you when you wake up tomorrow and you spend hours every day imagining what things that have yet to happen are gonna turn out like. I don't just mean winning the lottery; what about that hot date that you've got lined up after work, the season finale episode of your favourite show, that holiday you been waiting for, the result of that job interview last week...

You self-talk all the time about these kinds of things and there are only two kinds of people:

Those who talk to themselves and those who listen to themselves.

[Now if you're real smart you got that one from the jump. Did you? I knew you would. The rest of the class - just keep on thinking about it, you'll get there…]

Talk To Yourself, Not The Trees

The easiest way of all to practice acting - or indeed selling - is to talk to yourself. Yes, you heard me right. In a mirror. Yes, a mirror. Remember - who it is you spend the most time with again…? If you're uncomfortable using the phrase, "Talking To Yourself," due to the jacket-with-sleeves-that-tie-at-the-back implications then feel free to use the alternate term 'monologuing' [see *The Incredibles*].

This self-talk mirror exercise is a perfectly valid means of practising your side of the conversation with your prospect. Or any other conversation you want to rehearse, don't dismiss it. I mean it's not like you've never rehearsed something important you've wanted to say before, is it? Like a marriage proposal, for instance?

Or how about how to deliver those best lines of yours at that interview tomorrow? Never raged in your imagination at someone who has done you wrong as if they were actually stood in front of you, saying all those things you want to say to them without the problem of having them answer you back? No? Ok, that'll just be me then…

Mirror, Mirror On The Wall…

You know the saddest thing of all? The person I least want to see is in there looking back at me!

The person you spend the most time alone with is often the one you want to spend the least time alone with. When he talks too often you don't listen and when you do you disregard what he says. But like it or not you're stuck with him so the two of you may as well make the best of it and learn to get along with each other.

Actors must be self-aware and acting is just as much about knowing how what you're doing looks to an audience as it is about all the other stuff. If you're going to pull a funny face in order to get a laugh, then you need to know what that thing on the front of your head is going to look like when you do it. And how can you do that if you can't picture it in your own head? And how can you picture it if you've never seen it? Why do you think dance studios have floor to ceiling mirrors in them?

If you don't like what you see in the mirror, then your internal dialogue will reflect that. [Sorry, that was unintentional I promise...]

Robert Burns' Best Line! Ever!

"Oh wid the Lord the giftie gie us, to see oorsels as ithers see us!"

If we really could see ourselves as others see us, what would we see I wonder? And would we recognise it, never mind like it!

Just as you must be able to see your product from your prospect's perspective, so too must you see the product that is *you* from the point of view [POV] of the person who is going to be buying/employing you!

And think about the image you want to project, the version of *you* that you want them to see. How are you going to do that? With acting skills, maybe? That's where your time spent in front of the mirror talking to yourself, sorry monologuing, will come in so very useful. You can't be deceived if you know what it is the rest of the world sees.

Perfect Pitch?

If you want to learn the art of pitching, then check out the brave souls who venture into *The Dragon's Den*. It's a great show and we all love it when the Dragons turn them down, only for the follow-up show to reveal that they succeeded without them. At the same time we get an illicit thrill from watching those with more pride than ability come a cropper. The lesson of DD is this - your product is only as good as your ability to pitch it to a potential buyer. And remember, an actor is his own product!

Actors don't just do a quick bit of performing at an audition, they are pitching for the gig, asking a potential employer to invest in them instead of anyone else. With my writer's hat on, I know that the first hurdle you need to overcome is the initial pitching of your idea to the publisher, TV production company or movie studio. And when you try to sell your product to a prospect, you are pitching for their business too.

Mad Men

If you want to see The Art Of The Pitch in a dramatic context, then you could do no better than to check out *Mad Men* - not only is it a great TV show but there's a lot you can learn from watching Don Draper at work. The selective use of language, pacing a presentation, timing and vocal skills... it's all there for you to pick up on. And where do you think the writers got all that stuff from anyway?

Even if you're not an actor there's a lot you can learn from shows like *Mad Men*, *Dragon's Den* and *The Apprentice USA* . There are valuable lessons to be learned from watching others put their heads above the parapet, least of all how to dodge the bullets yourself when the time comes! It's a lot less painful to learn from other people's mistakes than it is to make them yourself...

Selling Your Self

An actor is his own product and, like any product, it needs a marketing strategy and a target audience. Actors themselves have very little control over the direction of their careers, as it's often in the hands of others - the ones who do the casting. But an actor owes it to himself to do all he can to maximise his chances by knowing the most effective way to market himself as a product in the arts marketplace.

As a seller, you know that people don't really buy products - they buy the person selling the product and the way that person makes them feel. They buy your conviction, and your enthusiasm, and your expertise, and your likeability. They buy you. You are no different from a politician or a preacher or an actor. You are a product yourself that you need to sell. But just how do you do that?

Buying The LIE

An actor is a person who appears natural in unnatural situations, like standing on the bridge of the Starship Enterprise, or fiddling with the controls of the TARDIS. But what is it about some actors that gets them work more consistently than the rest of their competitors? Why is it that in life the best person for the job, and by that I mean you and me, often doesn't get it? Why does it go to someone less talented, less able, instead?

Because the one thing people buy more than any other is a LIE:

A LIKEABLE INTERESTING EXPERT

And the kind of person who always seems to get ahead is a LIAR:

LIKEABLE INTERESTING AND REAL

Actors often talk about how the camera loves someone and if you watch reality TV shows you will see presenters whose personality seems to come right through the screen at you. Then there are others who, whilst competent enough, just don't seem to trigger the same sort of connection with the viewer. Why? What's the secret to connecting with an audience?

The Third Big Secret

There are certain actors and presenters who seem to have the ability to just connect instantly with an audience. Why? Because they are RAGs, that's why! And what's a RAG? Someone who comes across as

REAL AND GENUINE

They are the kind of people who generate enormous affection, the extent of which is often only made known after they're gone. And you need to be both a RAG and a LIAR if you are going to be The Best Seller You Can Be - that's our goal, remember.

Non-RAGs are those who are perfectly competent at what they do but don't seem to have a personality or self-expression that comes across as genuine. Actors and sellers both need to be relaxed and comfortable with who they really are. On TV, any artifice or performance for the camera will come across loud and clear to the audience at home. In a sales scenario, if your prospect thinks you are pretending to be interested in them just to get the sale, then you can virtually forget it. Being relaxed, real and genuinely expressive is what's really impressive.

Homework

Ok, you can see this one coming a mile off, can't you? I want you to spend as much time as you can stand talking to yourself in front of a mirror. I don't care what time of the day you do it, just make sure that you do it! Every day for a week preferably. Bathrooms are good places for this exercise as it's usually the only room in the house where you can be guaranteed some time alone, just the two of you...

You can start off by doing all that face-pulling stuff if you like but if you do, try this: pull a face and see how it looks in the mirror. Now look away and try to recreate it. Then look back and see how well you did. You can try all sorts of expressions, the idea is that you build up a mental picture of what it is your face is doing when you express yourself. [And if you feel really brave, try various emotive faces on your partner and see if they can guess which one it is you're meant to be doing. The results can often be hilarious if you both try it...]

But back to our exercise proper - talking to yourself.

You can take two approaches to this, either tell yourself all about the rotten day you've just had and get it all off your chest or tell yourself what you're going to do today or tomorrow and how you plan to make it happen. And if you really are too self-conscious to do this exercise then you really shouldn't be in sales. If you were slightly less self-conscious of course, you could tell yourself that in the mirror...

COMING UP IN CHAPTER 12...

We discover our first real life application of acting skills, Bryan shows us that often we are acting without realising it and Part One of the book comes to an end. See you there!

Bryan McCormack

CHAPTER TWELVE

BUT I CAN'T ACT!
OH YES YOU CAN!

You don't just find acting skills in the acting profession. You find them in other professions and walks of life too. In this final chapter of Part One we'll look at some of the people, other than actors, who have learned to use acting skills as selling tools.

So let's jump right in and highlight one very important principle that every seller needs to bear in mind when it comes to dealing with both prospects and customers...

Anyone can Act but not everyone is an Actor

Acting is something that anyone can do and as I will go on to show you everyone does it at some point in their lives. This form of acting is not the same thing as the kind of acting that will provide you with a living in television or in the West End, but it's just as valid. Remember what Stan The Man said about acting being realistic? Allied to that is the concept of being convincing. In exactly the same way that there are actors and people who can act...

There are Singers and people who can Sing

For instance, I can play the guitar but by no stretch of the imagination could I class myself as a guitarist. Oh I can pick out a tune and knock out some chords and string them together to make a song, but that's about it. Again, just because you can sing that doesn't make you a singer.

And as we've already seen, just because you have a talent for something, whatever field it's in, that alone is no guarantee of success.

There are many different types of acting that go on all around us every day, in all sorts of situations. For instance, acting and selling have more in common with politics and church than you might at first think.

The politician, the actor, the preacher and the seller all use the same basic skills in similar ways. Let's look at each of them in turn:

Politics

As someone who has been involved in UK Politics, albeit on a fairly minor level, I can assure you first hand that the reality really isn't that far removed from its portrayal in dramas like *House of Cards*, books like *First Among Equals* or even a comedy like *Yes Minister*.

Yes, some politicians could be labelled frustrated actors, but the truth is that they have learned the art of effective communication. Or, if you prefer, the doublespeak of answering the question without actually answering the question and leaving them with the impression that you did answer the question but nobody can remember what you said!

The politician spends more time in committee meetings than he does making speeches, though the public perception is that it's the other way round. Effective speechmaking is only one of several intersecting components required for political success and the art of oratory isn't what it used to be. Which, for people like me, is a shame.

Essentially a politician is a salesman. He is selling his party's policy on 'issue X' regardless of whether he actually agrees with it or not. [Debating skills are often best sharpened by having to argue for something you don't believe in!] The electorate are his customers.

But a politician is also an actor. He has to know his script - the party line on 'issue X' - and be able to deliver it in a convincing manner. It's also handy to be able to ad-lib when heckled during his performance by a journalist or member of the public!

Politicians are products and so are their parties. There are all sorts of PR, marketing and brand recognition issues that factor into political success or failure. But remember the TTC Principle - it's not always those who are the best who actually make it. And remember too, like any product, politics has a life cycle and tastes do change. I call this:

McCormack's Rule of Political Alternation

In the UK we tend to alternate our style of political leadership between two contrasting types - the Bank Manager and Mr Charisma.

Let's quickly look back over late 20th century prime ministers to prove the point. The process starts back in the 1960's with Harold Wilson.

Before Wilson came along every PM was a Bank Manager, with the singular possible exception of Churchill, for obvious reasons.

Harold Wilson was the first prime minister to really understand the power of television and ever since his successors - and their parties - have had to take account of its influence. They must understand not only how to use it to get their message across, but also how television makes them look. A voter's perception of reality is their reality and it is upon that reality - reality as they perceive it - that they will cast their vote.

As someone who has been interviewed about politics on live TV, I can assure you that I'd rather do acting any day! Of course it's very nice when the BBC phone you up and ask if you are free to go on the telly. [It's equally nice to have a BBC political editor's number on your mobile!]

But you appear as yourself and it's a completely different experience to being onstage. It can be very unnerving when you watch the recording and notice things about yourself, the real you, that you weren't previously aware of. That's probably why I'm a character actor instead of the other kind...

So, without further ado, here's the list:

- Harold Wilson - Mr Charisma
- Edward Heath - Bank Manager
- Harold Wilson [again] - Mr Charisma
- Jim Callaghan - Bank Manager
- Margaret Thatcher - Mr Charisma
- John Major - Bank Manager

- Tony Blair - Mr Charisma
- Gordon Brown - Bank Manager

Which means Gordon Brown will be replaced by a Mr Charisma figure when the time comes, whoever that may be... I can see no sign of this rule being broken in the immediate future but it serves to illustrate the point that everything - politically or otherwise - has a shelf life. When that product - politician or actor - reaches the end of its lifespan, then the public taste changes and so switches its allegiance to the exact opposite of what they're fed up with.

Political Alternation - American Style!

This rule of alternation also applies across the herring pond to The United States of America. Over there they alternate between Good Ole Boys and Rock Stars. As follows:

- John F Kennedy - Rock Star
- Lyndon Johnson - Good Ole Boy
- Richard Nixon - Rock Star
- Jimmy Carter - Good Ole Boy
- Ronald Reagan - Rock Star
- George Bush - Good Ole Boy
- Bill Clinton - Rock Star
- George W Bush - Good Ole Boy
- Barack Obama - Rock Star

Unless this rule is broken, the political Rock Star that is Barack Obama will eventually be replaced by a Good Ole Boy. Or maybe a Good Ole Girl. The UK has had a female Prime Minister but Uncle Sam is still waiting for the Commander-In-Chief they will call Madam President. And speaking of PMs...

Your MO and Your PM

We are all familiar I'm sure with the abbreviation MO which stands for Modus Operandi or Method of Operating, the way you do things. But you will be less familiar with what I call your PM, mainly because I've only just thought of it for this book!

Your PM is your PERSUASION MECHANISM

It's the thing you use to persuade your prospects to become customers. A politician is really nothing more than a professional persuader. Even those politicians who lack charisma - something that you would think would be a prerequisite for success - can get to the top. So they must be doing something effective to sell their product to the public. And as we've seen, a politician's product is not just his party, it's two interlinked things - policies and people.

Having great ideas on how the country should be run is one thing but it still comes down to the competency of the people who are going to put those policies into effect. That requires skills of both presentation and communication - skills actors already have and sellers need.

But remember the TTC Principle applies to politics as well as to acting and it also applies to selling too. So now let's leave the intrigues of The Westminster Village and The West Wing of the White House far behind, pretend it's Sunday and head on out to church!

Church

Preachers use the same skills that actors possess but for a slightly different purpose. Like politicians, not all of their job involves making speeches, or in this case sermons. Like a good speech, a good sermon has to engage it's audience, hold their attention and give 'em a couple of good laughs if possible.

More specifically, a sermon can either impart some spiritual insight, be evangelistic in nature or purely expository with some level of practical application. It will usually involve a quotation from The Bible [purely as an actor, I love The King James Version, it's right up there with dear old Billy Shakespeare's stuff for me] which is where a lot of otherwise good pulpit speakers come a cropper. The ability to speak well does not equate to a proportionate ability to read well.

So there are just a couple of examples of other areas of life where people can put acting skills to effective use. Preachers are taught in seminary how to construct a sermon [they even have books of pre-prepared ones if they can't think of their own!] and politicians are given media training. But the similarities don't end there...

Being an ASP

In a moment we're going to do a quick comparison between the four types of people we've looked at in this chapter - the actor, the preacher, the politician and the seller. But before we do I just want to point out that each of these people is an ASP. What's an ASP? It's an:

Acting Skills Practitioner

And you don't have to be an actor to be one, okay?

There are many more professions where you can see acting skills at work but for now we'll stick to these four. Now, ask yourself these four questions for each of the four ASPs:

1. What is their product?
2. Who are they promoting it to?
3. What is their persuasion mechanism?
4. How do they measure success?

	1	2	3	4
ACTOR	Himself	Audiences	Dialogue	Tickets/ Viewers
SELLER	Anything	Customers	Presentation	Total Sales
POLITICIAN	His Party	Electorate	Speeches/ Debate	Votes
PREACHER	His Beliefs	Congregation	Sermons	Converts

Can you see the similarities between the four of them? Why do you think I'm taking the time to point this out? I can assure you I do have a very good reason which we will come back to in Part Two!

All four ASP types have one thing in common, besides the obvious fact that they use the same skills for a different purpose. And that is… what?

An audience!

Working With An Audience

Every actor needs an audience, just as every seller needs customers. The one without the other will ensure you have a very short, stressful and profitless career. But if you are a seller, then you must realise that your customers are your audience. Just like the audience an actor plays to, your audience has to be entertained by a performance, in this case of superior salesmanship. An actor gets applause, you get sales.

Every actor, just like every seller, needs to find a market for his product. Products only fail for two reasons:

1. because they do not meet the basic MAN or SAP criteria,

2. the market is too small to sustain the product into profitability.

You can find a market for just about anything, but that market has to be big enough to make your product or service a profitable one. For the actor that market is his audience, whether in the theatre or on television or at the movies. You may have an unshakeable belief in your product, and you should, but if nobody's buying what you're selling then the best that you can say is that you've got something that not enough people want to make it worthwhile doing. At least professionally...

An audience is a curious thing, it takes on a sort of collective identity that you can actually discern when you're onstage. And the challenging thing is that every night is different. A gag that went down a storm on Monday night will fall flat on Tuesday. But that bit at the start of act two with the donkey and the whisky bottle, well they've never laughed at that before, but they did tonight.

Whenever you are interacting with someone else, regardless of the situation, if it's a sale or not, you are working an audience. And the way to work an audience is to get them onside. When an audience gives you its favour, then you're half way to your goal of convincing them that you are who you are pretending to be. As a seller, that's when you are more likely to gain the sale than to lose it. But beware, there are all sorts of pitfalls and bear traps out there, ready to catch the unwary who don't know what to do when things go wrong.

You are an Actor & you didn't even know it!

You are already using acting skills in different areas of your life without even realising it. And so are millions of others, every day. We've already talked quite a bit about acting but let's distil the essence of it in order to understand how people use it in everyday life. Then we'll move on to how you can use it more effectively to sell your product. But first...

Acting, as we have already seen is the business of pretending to be someone else. But there's a bit more to it than that. As an actor you must be convincing in the role you play, you must get the audience to believe that you really are the character you are playing [they can let you know how good they thought the real you was at the Curtain Call]. You will have heard the phrase 'suspension of disbelief'. This refers to the ability to draw your audience into the story, get them emotionally involved with it to the point where they forget that they are watching something, they are actually taking part in it.

Actors are convincers.

Sellers need to be convincers too.

The Convincibility Key

There is a world of difference between selling a thing and being the thing that you are selling. Here in the UK we've recently had a batch of TV shows to find someone to play a leading role in a West End musical:

Any Dream Will Do - Joseph and The Amazing Technicolour Dreamcoat

How Do You Solve A Problem Like Maria - The Sound Of Music

I'd Do Anything - Oliver!

What was it about the winners of those shows that got them the part ahead of their rivals? Were they more talented? Did they have a better voice? Were they a better actress than a singer? If you voted in any of those shows, you will have had a reason for preferring one contestant over another. What was it?

CONVINCIBILITY - the persuasive ability to make someone sure or certain of something.

Like, "I am THE perfect casting for this Role" or,

"This is THE product for you!" [And aren't you glad I sold it to you!]

Anything you want to achieve that requires the agreement of someone else requires you to max out your convincibility quotient.

So actors are convincers. Can you think of any times in your own life where you've had to convince anyone?

Go On - Convince Me!

What about a job interview? The person doing the interviewing doesn't see the real you because that's not who's sitting in front of them, is it?

No, it's *you on your best day*, the you that's suited and booted, saying all the right things to make a good impression and convince the person opposite that they should give the job to *you* and not the competition.

What about chatting someone up in the pub? Again, they don't see you, they see a version of you that's looking good and smelling great, oozing attractiveness from every pore, sharply dressed and saying all the right things to convince her to go out with *you* and not the competition.

[I suppose selling can be seen as a form of seduction, maybe acting too come to that...]

Over on the dark side, what about trying to convince that traffic cop not to give you a ticket? He's not seeing the real you, he's seeing *you at your nicest, most humble and most apologetic.*

Or what about all those times you've phoned in sick to work just so you could get a duvet day...?

Or hardest of all, explaining to your wife where you've been all night! [Some gigs are tougher than others...]

I suppose you could say actors are nothing more than professional liars. On those terms pretending to be someone else could be classed as lying convincingly. Well now, if you can use your ability to lie convincingly in the kind of social situations given in the preceding examples, why then can't you use that ability to convince your prospect to buy your product?

All you're really doing is what actors do - convincing someone of something that's not really true. You don't actually have to believe in the features and benefits of a product to be able to sell it effectively and professionally. And if you can be deceptively convincing in real-life situations like those in the examples above then, with some effective direction from Part Two of this book, you are all set to become that Best Seller You Always Wanted To Be!

See you in Part Two!

Bryan McCormack

INTERMISSION

Okay, this is the point where we stop, take a breather and gather our thoughts from Part One. I've shared a lot of information with you and you owe it to yourself to take the time to make sure you understand all of it. So look on this part of the book as the equivalent of an interval in the theatre. Or, if you ever saw *Chitty Chitty Bang Bang* in the cinema, as the moment where the car goes over the cliff!

I'm going to recap some of the main points I've given you so far, the ones that I think are really important for you to bear in mind as we get ready to move forward into Part Two - Selling and Acting. OK, here goes:

- ESP - Everyone Sells a Product
- What does a product do? Meets A Need, Solves A Problem
- Two kinds of actors - character and personality
- Acting is a business! Actor for sale!
- Acting is…? #1 - Intellect and Emotion
- Acting is…? #2 - pretending to be someone else
- Inflexibility leads to fatality
- What is an ACTOR?
    o Action Creation Tension Observation Reaction
- What is ACTING?
    o Action Creation Tension Investigation Negation Generation
- The truth about acting - talent is not enough!

- What is talent? The natural ability to do something well
- TALENT is something that you have
- ABILITY is something that you learn
- SKILL is something you develop
- Talent should be PRACTICAL and
- PERSONAL - It's WHO you are
- PROFITABLE - It gets RESULTS for you
- PLEASUREABLE - It SATISFIES you
- PURPOSEFUL - It's WHY you are who you are!
- The Triangle of Triumph:
  - o Talent, Timing and Connections
  - o [Acting] TALENT - the natural ability to perform; to engage, entertain and convince an audience.
  - o TIMING - the capacity to discern the moment of maximum impact
  - o CONNECTIONS - customers for your Talent.
- The TTC Principle
- Talent + Timing + Connections = Opportunity!
- OPPORTUNITIES - temporary times of optimum advantage due to favourable conditions.
- ADVANTAGE - a unique attribute that advances your talent
- CONVERGENCE - when everything comes together just right
- An ACTOR is a marketable commodity in a competitive marketplace. An Actor is his own product.

- Remember You're A PRIAM :
  - o   Product Retailing In A Marketplace
- ARID #1 - Action Reaction Interaction Decision
- MADNESS - do the same thing expecting a different result
- ARID #2 - Adaptive Responses Initiate Differences
- Internal Dialogue - talk to yourself
- Anyone can act but not everyone is an actor
- Every product has a shelf life
- Your PM - Persuasion Mechanism
- ASP - Acting Skills Practitioner
- Work with your audience and get their favour
- You are an actor and you didn't even know it!
- Actors are convincers. Sellers need to be convincers too.
- Convincibility - the persuasive ability to make someone sure or certain of something
- LIE - Likeable Interesting Expert
- LIAR - Likeable Interesting And Real
- RAG - Real And Genuine

Bryan McCormack

ACT TWO &
BEGINNERS PLEASE!

1. INT. THE THEATRE. BAR.

The Audience are chatting to each other, exchanging views and evaluating the first half of the show. Then, from the Public Address System:

ANNOUNCER: Ladies and Gentlemen, tonight's performance of "Sell Yourself: Act Your Way To Sales Success", will continue shortly in the main auditorium. Please return to your seats.

2. INT. CONTROL GALLERY.

The TV DIRECTOR checks his Shooting Script.

Ok, stand by Studio. Ready to go Live. Act Two.

3.INT. DRESSING ROOM.

Our Hero is resting, relaxing with some Alexander Technique, ready for the second half. Then from the TANNOY on the wall:

TANNOY VOICE: Act Two & Beginners please. Act Two & Beginners to the stage. Mr McCormack, this is your Call. Good luck everyone.

Our Hero stands, ready to go back out and face his audience. With a last look in the mirror, he EXITS

4. INT. THE WINGS.

Our Hero ENTERS and presses the Call Button on the wall, signalling to the Stage Manager that he is in position.

5. INT. THE THEATRE.

The AUDIENCE are settling themselves. The LIGHTS in the auditorium begin to DIM. An excited air of ANTICIPATION!

6. INT. THE WINGS.

The Cue Light turns GREEN and Our Hero returns onstage to THUNDEROUS APPLAUSE!

And - Camera One!

SELL YOUR SELF!

Act Your Way To Sales Success!

BRYAN McCORMACK

ACT TWO - SELLING & ACTING

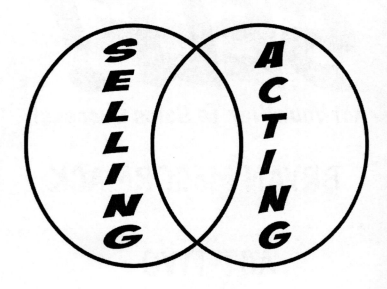

CHAPTER THIRTEEN

PEOPLE WHO EAT PEOPLE...

...are the yuckiest people in the world! In Part One we looked at acting skills and demonstrated why they are important to sellers. In Part Two I'm going to show you how you can use those acting skills as selling tools. Before we do that though, there is one important topic we need to cover first:

The Problem of People

Actors are nothing without an audience, just as sellers are nothing without customers. Both those targets for our talent are made up of people and they are the biggest obstacle to our success.

You'll never successfully sell to people unless you understand how they work, what makes them tick, why they are the way they are. If you're going to get the most out of this second section of the book I need to be upfront with you about my views on your customers, who I think they really are and what I think they're really like. So let's kick off with something fairly familiar:

The Onion Analogy

An old [and incomplete] definition of acting was "a synthesis between the heart, the mind and the will". I prefer to take the spirit, soul and body approach instead, which is this:

You are a spirit, you have a soul and you live in a body.

I am utterly convinced by a combination of reason, research and personal experience that human beings are triune in nature - they have three layers. So yes, Shrek was right. The outermost layer is your physical body; that's what we see of you. [And yes, we all know we shouldn't judge a book by its cover but it's a fact that our modern society is guilty of this more than ever. You'll just have to deal with it as best you can.]

The next layer is your soul, which is made up of your mind, will and emotions [more about that in a minute]. The innermost layer - or core - is your spirit. This is the real you. If it helps, think of planet earth - science tells us it has a core [spirit], an inner mantle [soul] and a surface [body - bit obvious, that last one!].

Head & Heart

Now I realise that you may disagree vehemently with me on this [and no, I'm not into all that new age nonsense either] but that's ok, you're allowed. If you think that human beings are nothing more than a random collection of chemical reactions inside a neurological network then fine, that's up to you. Go have a happy life. But don't expect me to agree with you. Sorry, but you're way too late for me!

Some people prefer the simpler notion of head and heart - that you are a combination of what you think and what you feel. If that's what works for you then I'm happy for you. [But be happy for me too, ok?]

Breaking The Belief Barrier

You may be asking why am I telling you this? Because people always act on what they believe. And people's actions will always correspond to their belief system, whatever that is. My view of what people are really like is the basis for what I'm about to teach you in the rest of the book.

You need to understand where I'm coming from if you are going to be able to take these upcoming principles and successfully apply them yourself in your own selling scenarios.

I have nothing to gain from not telling you the truth as I see it.

For example, let's suppose that you believe in the existence of God and I believe in the non-existence of God. We believe different things but we both believe in something! Trouble is, too often people aren't content to agree to disagree. Opposing belief systems are too often barriers to two people connecting because, although there is a natural submission in people, there is also a contradictory desire to dominate.

As a seller, you must be able to appear to convincingly connect to your prospect's belief system, even if you personally disagree with it. I mean, do you want their money or not?

Those among you with some smarts will have realised that I have just done something which most sellers miss completely. I have, in fact, been doing it throughout the book thus far. Do you know what it is? If you do, then well done - you're one up on a lot of the sellers I've met. [Don't worry I'll let the rest of them in on our secret later!]

Spirit, Soul & Body

Your body is the thing that your spirit and your soul use to express themselves. Your body is the vehicle by which your soul and spirit interact with other souls and spirits - potential customers - in the physical dimension of reality. As an actor I use a physical medium to express an emotional and intellectual message - what's in my heart and in my head [and sellers do the same thing when interacting with customers]. In this instance I'm writing it - the message - down, but I could just as easily record an audio version of this text and still convey the same message via a different end medium but I would still have to use my physical body to express what I'm thinking [head] and want to say [heart].

Selling Your Soul

So your body - your outermost layer - is the means by which you act out the message of what it is you're acting out. But what about the next layer down, your soul?

Your soul is made up of your mind [intellect], will [choice] and emotions [feelings]. When it comes to either performing a play or filming a movie, as an actor you use your mind to understand the text and what the author wants to say. With your heart you express the emotions needed to bring those words to life. Your will is what chooses to take a risk and propels you out onstage or onscreen to bring the author's message to life.

But What About...

Now you may say, "Oi! What about the Ego and the Id and the conscious and subconscious and all that stuff?" Well here are two very good reasons for not mentioning "all that stuff":

1. I don't have a degree in psychology so wouldn't know what I was talking about if I did mention them, meaning I would have to bluff my way with something cribbed off Wikipedia - and I'm not going to do that.

2. I stick to what I know. I know about acting and selling and people. People [and ogres!] are like onions, they have layers. Deal with it.

[And finally, remember this - new age stuff is big business. Some people are looking for evidence of a spiritual dimension to life. Some of those people are your potential customers. Moving on...]

Time for a Reality Check

In my world, the reality is it's a simple choice between two opposing views of human nature.

Either:

> People are essentially good but simultaneously capable of bad things,

Or,

> People are essentially bad but simultaneously capable of good things.

Sadly I am compelled to conclude that it's the latter. You may disagree with me. Fine, that's your choice and your right. But you'd be wrong if you did. Knowing that people are essentially selfish in nature but capable of selflessness means you are less likely to get ripped off, taken for a ride or completely screwed. By all means always look on the bright side of life but it pays to be a realist. Particularly in business. The cynic in me says a friend is someone who won't stab you in the back unless he really has to...

Negativity Comes Naturally

But that doesn't mean you have to accept it as your nature. You still have a choice in how you react to the negative circumstances you may find yourself in. Darkness is, after all, only the absence of light...

Remember the old parable about the two identical houses? One built on the sand and the other built on the rock? A storm came along and destroyed the house built on the sand but the house built on the rock remained. The message is that it's your foundation that determines whether or not you'll still be standing when the storms of life hit you. But there's another aspect to this that most people miss and it's this...

It was the same storm that hit both houses! The right foundation - a solid belief system in other words - will see you through the storm but it is no guarantee that your life will be storm-free. And the determining factor in surviving any of life's storms is your attitude towards it.

Beware The People Eaters!

We can all recall times where we've been used, ripped off, conned, taken for a ride etc - chewed up and spat out by The People Eaters of this world, folks who get off on messing up other people's lives, if not ending them outright. The nightly news is full of 'em. Most social devouring is more insidious though, you know the kind of thing. The parent who's always putting you down, the possessive boyfriend/girlfriend, the selfish neighbour next door who insists on partying 'til 3am, the barking dog that belongs to an inconsiderate owner...

Worst of all though, are those social vampires who just suck all the life out of you, toxic friends who just bring you down every time you get around them. They usually have a problem they just can't get over - like being dumped - and each time they rehearse their problem instead of dealing with it they get more wearing to be around. You get to the place where you no longer enjoy their company and finally you start to avoid them. On purpose. Word of advice - the minute one of your friends turns toxic, just think *Shaun of the Dead* and run for your life! And speaking of life, let me finish by telling you about...

The Seven Spheres

Celebrities love to talk about having their 'private life' invaded, when they've just sold their wedding, honeymoon and first argument for squillions of pounds - complete with pictures. Although it always makes the cynic in me smile, there is an important principle at work in this kind of thinking and it's called compartmentalisation. Here's how it works:

Because men's brains are wired differently from women's, a man finds it easy to separate his thoughts from his feeling [that's the main reason for pornography] whereas a woman always makes all her decisions with her emotions involved. But both of them view their life as being made up of different components - they have their work life, their home life, their social life, their family life and their sex life.

Just as we each individually regard our lives as having components or areas where different activities take place, in the same way you can regard human life in general as being made up of different areas or spheres or components. How many can you think of?

Well obviously there's sales and acting for a start. Then there's politics...

Ok, to save time I've listed what are generally regarded as the seven key spheres of human activity. And here they are:

1. The family
2. Education
3. The arts
4. Media
5. Government
6. Business
7. Church

Think of your life as a pie chart which has a greater or lesser percentage given over to those spheres that you're active in. Here's what it might look like for someone like me:

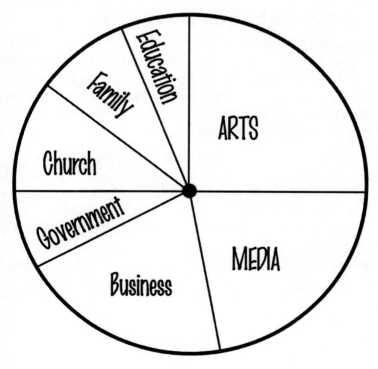

Obviously I'm most active in the arts and media spheres but I'm also increasingly active in the business sphere too. You may sell your product in the government sphere or the education sphere. Although I've been politically active in my time I didn't go to University so the government and education spheres play very little part in my life at present.

However you divide up your life's pie chart, remember that there are others who will divide theirs up differently to yours. This is where...

The Advantage of Being Everyman...

...comes in. The advantage being that you can talk to anyone, on any level, in any social situation. An actor is lost without this skill and I'm happy to say that it's an ability I am blessed to possess in abundance. In each of those seven spheres I just mentioned there are potential customers for you and your product.

If you are going to make serious money from selling you cannot afford to be inactive or uncomfortable in any of those areas. Sure you may have to bluff your way in some more than others but everyone has an opinion and if your own is a bit fuzzy then turn the tables and ask them what their opinion is. [It's always a good idea to get people talking about their favourite subject - themselves!]

Homework

Draw a circle on a blank sheet of paper and divide up your own life using the seven spheres I mentioned, apportioning each what you think is the right proportion of time, attention, experience and energy they currently occupy in your life. Which areas are your strongest? Your weakest? Which are too big? Too small? Which spheres do you have contacts in? Are there any spheres that you have no contacts in? Are there customers for your product in those spheres that you are not currently reaching? If so, what do you think you could do about it?

COMING UP IN CHAPTER 14...

Bryan shows you the first step to becoming a super seller and explains all about what your SPI index is and why it matters to your selling career. See you there!

CHAPTER FOURTEEN

HOW TO BE A SUPER SELLER

Now that we've got the nasty but necessary business of dissecting your customers out of the way, let's move on to the really fun part - sellers and what makes them tick! Here in Part Two of the book we're going to deconstruct the classic sales process and show you the secret to making it work more effectively than ever before. You will learn some acting skills that you can use in a very practical way to make the most of every single prospect and convert more of them into customers.

But before we get into that, there are a few very important points you need to remember. And here is the first:

Nobody else can sell like you do

Each of us is unique. We all have our own personality and our own way of expressing it. Each of us is physically unlike anyone else, even if we are similar in height and build. Even identical twins are not entirely identical. Our voice is unique to us and even the best impressionist cannot replicate it exactly. There is no-one like you on the entire planet!

Your uniqueness also applies to the way you sell. You may learn a standard sales technique but the way you apply and express that will be unique to you. This explains:

Why you can't sell like I do

You are not me and I am not you. We both have a completely unique history of experiences that go to make up the individual expression of our singular personality. We bring all that to bear in our selling. Our own way of implementing our PM is exactly that - our own. If I see or hear you do something that works for you, I can't then go out and replicate that exactly and expect it to work. It will remain your technique, not mine and it'll be as false as an impressionist on the TV. We all know who they're meant to be, but they're not the real thing.

Sell Your Self Like You Would Sell Yourself

The real problem with a lot of the "How To..." stuff out there is that it sets itself up as some hard and fast rule that must be applied regardless. Sorry, but that's simply not true. You need to find your own way through the jungle of techniques and possibilities. I am sharing with you what works for me and why I believe it will work for you too, but how it works for you is up to you. You have to take the principles I'm sharing and personalise them. If you think you can improve on what I've given you then feel free to go right ahead and try and do it better. [And if it works, let me know for the Fully Revised and Updated version, ok?]

When I was a team leader, I always told my agents to find their own way of selling our client's product. I would demonstrate how I did it. But they would still have to take that principle and find a way to make it their own using their own personality and expression. In the same way, I would watch how others made sales and take those elements that I thought were usable for me. Of course the advantage I had was that I was an actor and could be pretty much anyone I wanted to be, depending on who I was talking to. Flexibility and adaptability, that's the name of the game. However, the truth is:

You Really Need To Stop Selling!

You really do. And the sooner you can stop selling the easier it will be for you to get sales. And then you will get bigger sales. And bigger rewards.

You see - I have never sold a single product in my entire selling career.

Not one.

When I sold anything, I did something which none of my competitors did. What I did when I was selling was unique to me and as far as I could see, no-one else was doing it. When I looked around I couldn't find anyone who was teaching what I did as an effective sales tool. That's why I wrote this book. Not everyone will know what you are about to learn. Which is this:

Can You Keep A Secret?

Sell in character, not as yourself.

Create a sales character and let him do the selling.

Acting is selling and selling is acting. I've already proved to you that you can act in ordinary everyday situations so there's no reason why you can't act equally convincingly in a sales situation, is there? Of course not. And there's one huge benefit to this approach which alone makes it worth doing. [We'll cover that in the next chapter.] So what I'm going to do is show you how to construct a sales character, one that suits who you are, your personality and selling style. But before I do that:

The Universality Factor

We talked in chapter 12 about ASPs. [You do remember what an ASP is don't you? Acting Skills Practitioner, ok?] Well here's the insight that I was hinting at earlier, which you may not have cottoned onto at the time:

Everyone is an ASP.

And I do mean EVERYONE! Including YOU!

This universality factor should be a great relief to you. It means you can stop torturing yourself that you're just not suited to sales, you're not a natural, it's not who you are, all of that nonsense. None of it's true.

Everyone is an ASP because every day we are alive we all pretend to agree with people we don't agree with, like things we don't like and enjoy doing things we detest. We all use acting skills in all sorts of everyday situations to convince others that we are genuine when we are not. There is no reason why, as an already self-confident seller, that you cannot add those same skills to your sellers toolkit.

Superheroes & Alter-Egos

So we're going to construct a sales character that you will use when you sell. So take some time to think about who this sales character might be. I want you to think, initially at least, in terms of comic book heroes who all have alter-egos to hide their true identity.

Clark Kent is really Superman, Spiderman is really Peter Parker, Batman is really Bruce Wayne. So let us take *you* and assume that you are going to be Clark or Peter or Bruce. What is your Superman going to look like? Your Batman, your Spiderman? Who is your Sales Superhero? It doesn't have to be a comic book character but for the moment that is where we will start. Or, coming bang up to date, what about Mr Incredible? You can pick either the red or blue version, it's up to you.

OK, got one? Good. Now put the book down for five, ten minutes and think about how they would sell. I'll be here when you get back.

Hello there! Back so soon? That was quick, are you sure you didn't just skip that part and headed on over here anyway? Cutting corners, eh...

Ok, so now you've got the notion I want to talk about one of the benefits of succeeding as a seller - prosperity. This isn't always money but for our purposes it is. So let's take a look at:

Your SPI Index

This is a measure of how much of each of the following three PEs - Prosperity Elements - you have available to you in your own life. These three elements are:

Status, Power & Influence

Think about it. If you are prospering financially, it brings you a degree of each of these things. But how much of these, if any, do you currently have? And if we want to talk motivationally, how much of these three things would you like to have? To illustrate, let's think of three people who can demonstrate the differing balances of these three prosperity elements. Let's start with:

STATUS - HM THE QUEEN

If status is all about your rank or standing in society then, as Head of State, the Monarch enjoys enormous status and some considerable influence but she has very little real power.

POWER - THE PRIME MINISTER

The PM has a great deal of power [and patronage] a fair bit of status - but not as much as the monarch, and only while he's in the job - and a fair bit of influence too.

INFLUENCE - SIR HUMPHREY

The Whitehall Mandarins - now forever known as Sir Humphreys thanks to *Yes, Minister* - have enormous Influence as permanent civil servants to temporary and alternating governments. They have some status, but only amongst other members of the service, and a fair bit of power.

148

So we have three people, all with differing levels of SPI - Status, Power and Influence in different proportions. I leave it up to you to decide which of the three ultimately comes out on top, but it's probably the PM.

Growing Into Your Goals

The main thing that held me back when I started out as an actor was a lack of ambition. I was naïve enough to think that my talent would be enough and all I really wanted to do was keep working. Partly I can blame my parents for not instilling any sort of ambition in me when I was a child but I have to take responsibility for my actions too.

If you lack a clear purpose and an achievable goal, the more fuzzy and out of focus your future seems to you, then the harder it will be to navigate your way through your future. Life is a sequence of bifurcation points - forks in the road - and the reason too many people go wrong is that they don't stop and think about the consequences of their actions. That's not to say you shouldn't consider the risks with any big choice, but those risks still have to be taken.

[Risks are much easier to take if you have a clear idea of why you're taking that risk. The potential rewards of that opportunity - don't forget about the TTC principle! - help you to deal with any unintended consequences that may result from your failing to pull it off.]

Future Times Past

Who you are now is a result of the choices you've made up to now. There's the *Old You*, there's *You Now* and the

New You that you're going to become. That New You, will be a result of the choices you're going to make. So it makes sense to have a clear idea of *who you want to be* before you start, don't you think?

Remember our Triangle of Fire from chapter 8 and how we used that as the basis of our Triangle of Triumph? Well in a minute we're going to use that again, but this time we're going to illustrate the difference between the *You Now* and the *New You*.

But first I want to quickly give you an alternate illustration to think about from *Doctor Who*. The first actor to play the role - in 1963 - was William Hartnell. He was followed three years later by Patrick Troughton and then in 1970 Jon Pertwee took over. This was when I started watching the show [*The Sea Devils* in 1972 if you want to know] and I'm proud to say I've never hid behind a sofa in my life! I was always on the edge of my seat instead. If I'm honest, the idea of playing at being The Doctor - and getting paid for it! - is what inspired me to be an actor in the first place!

These three actors - Hartnell, Troughton and Pertwee - appeared together in a tenth anniversary story called *The Three Doctors*. [Pertwee and Hartnell had previously appeared together in the 1953 film *Will Any Gentleman?*] Within the context of the story [available on BBC DVD] you have three different versions of the same person present at the same time, all seeing themselves from different viewpoints.

Dr #3 is meeting his past, Dr #1 is seeing his future and Dr #2 can see both his past and his future. Most people are like Dr #3, focussing too much on the past. There are very few people like Dr#1 that I've met, who are totally focussed on the future. I think the best place to be is in Dr #2's position, where you can see both ends of the spectrum of your life.

When I look back on the person I used to be, I don't recognise him. I'm not even that sure that I like him that much, if anything I think I feel sorry for him. But at the same time I want to slap him and tell him to stop being so green and get his act together. I'm sure most people could tell a similar story, or is that just me?

The PIG & The PIT

Ok, I'm gonna call this one The Triangle of Time, mainly because The Triangle of Personal Growth is too naff for words. It's the difference between *You Now* and the *New You* [Dr #2 and Dr #3 if you like].

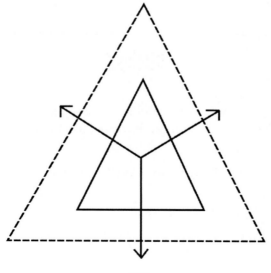

151

The inner triangle is *You Now*, the larger outer triangle is the person you are going to grow into, the *New You*. So here is the PIG version of the three growth elements you need to see your future before it happens:

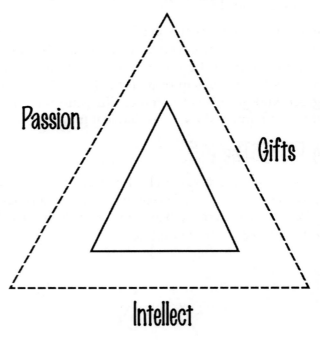

Your passion fires your intellect to seek out ways to use your gifts in a way that feeds your passion which fires your intellect… etc

Ok, here's the PIT version. Take your pick.

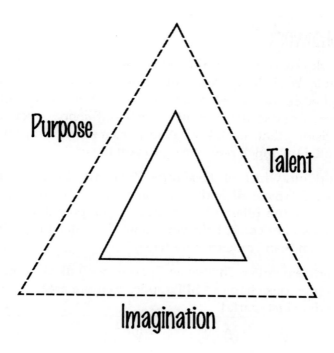

Your purpose feeds your imagination with things your talent can do to fulfil your purpose which feeds your imagination... etc

Old You, You Now or *New You* - you choose!

Homework

Work out your own SPI Index and that of your chosen comic book hero sales character. Who will have the higher rating? How much status do you have within your organisation? How much influence over the decisions that are taken? And perhaps most important of all, how much real power do you have?

Work out which of these three Prosperity Elements you have the most of and work on ways to increase your stock of the other two. Perhaps your potential acting skills ability could help you attain a greater proportion of them than you currently have?

[And remember The Seven Spheres we talked about in the previous chapter - SPI applies to more areas of your life than just work!]

COMING UP IN CHAPTER 15...

We see why developing a sales character is so important as Bryan gives us the secret to defeating a Superhero seller's greatest enemy - rejection! See you there!

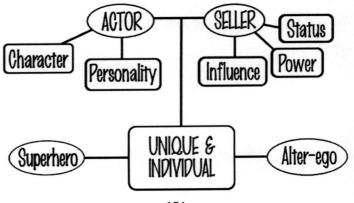

CHAPTER FIFTEEN

REFLECTIONS ON REJECTION

People are essentially bad but simultaneously capable of good things. The world in which we live is steeped in negativity. People find it really easy to be negative, as if it comes naturally. In our hectic, modern-day society, negativity is the norm. If you doubt that then you probably won't get much out of this chapter but read it anyway, just for me. Thanks.

I can't handle Rejection

Rejection is part of life. Some people get more of it than others and some people can handle it better than others. But there's a world of difference between having a coping strategy for when it strikes and being able to deflect it and stop it wounding you in the first place.

Some people get so much rejection in their lives that they in turn end up rejecting people before they reject them. They find themselves trapped in a cycle that they lack the emotional strength to break. I was one of them.

What you need to know about Rejection

They always tell you not to take rejection personally but that's not as easy to do as it is for them to say. Rejection is a message to your soul that says you're not wanted, you're not good enough, you don't meet the required standard. Everybody gets a measure of it in their lives, whether it's asking someone out and them saying no or applying to drama school and not getting in!

Think back over some of the rejections you've suffered - no, that's the wrong word - experienced in your own life. How did you handle those rejections? What was the message that you received from them?

Nobody gets every job that they apply for, especially actors. It goes with the territory. You expect it. For most people, rejection is not an accepted part of their chosen profession. Most people will go for a promotion and not get it maybe once or twice in their career and that's it. An actor has to deal with that possibility every single day. We know better than anyone how to handle rejection.

Rejection can be positive - it is a message to your soul that says, "if you really want this, you will have to improve if you are going to get it!"

Toxic Emotions

But because people are naturally negative, they don't receive that message when they experience rejection. They see it as a confirmation that they're unworthy or inferior. To them the message is, "you're never going to get this because you're not good enough. Just forget it!"

Because people are naturally negative, they naturally have a negative expectation. Ever heard any of these?

"It won't work, but I'll try it anyway."

"Nothing ever works for me."

"It's alright for you…"

Experience tells me that people will always act on what they believe. And they will believe themselves before they believe you or me.

What Goes In Is What Comes Out

Another thing I've learned over the years is this: what comes out of people is what's inside them. If they're filled with negativity, they will speak negatively. If nothing positive is coming out of them, it's because there's nothing positive in them! Listen to the words that your friends speak in the conversations that go on around you and ask yourself why are they saying those things? [Your friends are more likely to be genuine in what they say when they're relaxed and in familiar company.]

The important thing to remember is this:

If it ain't coming out of 'em, it ain't in there!

Purposeful Positivity

A newborn child is a blank canvas that life's experiences will write on. Success in life is not a matter of genetics - that's just a convenient excuse for failure and the perpetuation of a victim mentality - it's a matter of upbringing and personal choice.

Two people can face the same crisis but only one of them will come through it unscathed. Why? Attitude. Just because we live in a world that surrounds us with negativity, that doesn't mean we have to be negative. You can be positive on purpose. Think of those people you have known who always seem to be on the 'up' escalator of life, the people who seem to lift your spirits when you meet them. We need more people like that!

Efficient Living

As well as being positive on purpose, you need to be efficient in your life. By that I mean stop doing things unless they return a profit on your investment of time, effort and energy. Only do those things that are going to give you results or satisfaction or pleasure - not that you should seek those things just for the sake of it but understand that most people's real motive is a self-serving one. You love you more than anyone else on the planet. How do you like the idea of a life where you only do things you enjoy? Sounds good to me! That's everyone's innermost dream - to only do what they enjoy doing. Maximum return for the minimum effort is efficiency. We look to make a return on our financial investments but forget to apply this same principle to our everyday living.

If, like me, you've ever worked in a call centre, you will know that efficiency is one of your KPIs or Key Performance Indicators. Efficiency targets are always set in excess of 90%. In one of my workplaces the efficiency target was 96%, which meant that 96% of my working day should be spent on the phones doing my job selling the client's product. The other 4% - working out at about 18 minutes - was allowed for things like one-to-one reviews, team briefings etc. [Though most agents were under the mistaken impression that it meant they had an entitlement to an 18-minute paid toilet break...]

As managers, we were encouraged to see our part of the business as our own business. There were five of us and each team was treated as if it were a little company in its own right. There was no way I was going to spend money on wages for agents who were inefficient - especially when I was the first to arrive and the last to leave! My team may not have had the most sales but we were consistently the most efficient!

Authorising Authority

All authority systems look for maximum effort for minimum return from those who are subordinate to it. And hard work is not always the best paid - just look at our modern 'celebrity' society and you can see that. Governments of all political persuasions are inefficient, bureaucratic, wasteful, dictatorial and play on people's natural inbuilt submission to authority, otherwise society would collapse into anarchy. [Ever heard of a bloke by the name of Dr Joseph Juran? Nope, neither had I until recently. He came up with the phrase, "the vital few and the trivial many", which pretty much sums up how elites of all kinds view the rest of us plebs.]

Another way of expressing that is what's termed The Hegelian Dialectic. The German philosopher Hegel's idea was that all historical events arise out of conflict. [And what's the essence of drama again? Yup, conflict!] You have two opposing groups, bosses and workers for example, which he termed thesis and antithesis. You then let them play out their conflict and resolve the resultant tension by the imposition of a solution, which he called synthesis. The thing about Hegel is that his idea works equally well if the people who provide the solution are the same ones who caused the problem in the first place!

So the authority systems of this world demand maximum effort from you and give you a minimum return... in return. You need to start to turn that around in your life and get the system to give you a maximum return for a minimum of effort. No government of any political persuasion can be trusted because power corrupts and that leads to a government that exists to impose its will on the people not implement the will of the people.

And the bigger a government gets the more inefficient it becomes. It's a fact that people take better care of their own stuff than other people's, which is why really prosperous people are smart enough to pay a clever accountant to help them minimise their tax bill... This leads us to:

Pareto's Principle

I had heard this principle many times over the years before I finally found out who it was credited to, a bloke called Vilfredo Pareto. Fredo noticed that 20% of the people owned 80% of the wealth. [For many years in Scotland there was a left-wing socialist theatre company called 7: 84 which worked on the same principle, though obviously they viewed the split in different proportions.]

As a seller I've often heard it said that 20% of your customers supply 80% of your sales. I've also heard it said that 20% of your business accounts for 80% of its running costs. If this truly is a universally applicable principle then that means that only 20% of what you do will result in 80% of your success. So it looks like it pays to be efficient!

Inside Out Living

Never underestimate the power of a life lived inside out, a life that spends it's time radiating positivity to others rather than spending it's time dealing with what others project onto them.

The principle of sowing and reaping - that you get what you give - is as good a way to live your life as any. And for a seller like you and an actor like me, it's the only sensible lifestyle choice on offer. Everyone you meet is a potential customer for your product so can you really afford to go around upsetting or teeing off anybody? And I do mean anybody, because you never know who's watching you that you can't see. Or who's overhearing you that you're not aware of. Until it's too late.

If you are positive on purpose you are putting credits in the bank that you may very well have to draw on in the future. Think of it as your goodwill pension. You pay money into a monetary pension, so pay goodwill into your goodwill pension. I find that easier than that whole thing about paying it forward which is just too clunky for me.

People like to buy from nice, smiley, happy people, not nasty, mean, grumpy people. So be nice to everyone you meet, if humanly possible. And if not, just hope that no potential customers get to hear about it!

I Expected To Be Rejected

When I was a teenager I was isolated, lonely and desperate for a girlfriend. I had a history of rejection which set up a pattern of negative expectation in my life. So when a friend of mine and his girlfriend set me up with a girl who actually fancied me, you can guess what happened.

Because I expected to be rejected, I was always on the defensive when it came to girls and did what all defensives do. I got my rejection in first. Do it to them before they do it to you. Looking back, it was of course complete lunacy - I was cutting myself off from the very thing I was reaching out for! But wounded people with negative expectations aren't rational - they're trapped in a cycle of self-deception which is hard, but not impossible, to break. It's hard to exude positivity when there's little that's positive in your life. [But then again, that's a question of attitude too. One storm, two houses, remember?]

Have you ever heard the expression "hurting people hurt people"? Well that described me to a tee. I expected to be rejected so I rejected first and then when they rejected me I could turn round to myself and say I told you so and retreat into my shell again and reinforce that same SDB. [SDBs are Self Destructive Behaviours and they can be deadly. I know!]

Who Would Buy You?

There I was, at my mate's house. There's me and his girlfriend, having a quiet drink. [This is back in the late eighties.] The doorbell goes and there takes place a rather unconvincing, "I wonder who that could be... oh hello, what a surprise!" type conversation followed by, "look who's here!" and in walks this poor girl that we'll call Carol.

Now I knew Carol from the local AmDram and yes, she was quite attractive as I recall. But there was no way I would ever have had the courage to ask her out. By the time I realised I had been set up I was in maximum self-defence mode, the emotional drawbridge was up and there was no way anyone was getting in. [I was in my early twenties.]

Well poor old Carol, I don't know what she must have thought. I can't remember exactly what I said - it was nearly thirty years ago - but we can both have a pretty good guess. When she finally got up to leave she made one last try and offered me a lift home, which I politely but very firmly declined. Needless to say the look on my mate's girlfriend's face when Carol had gone was a picture. And as for what she said to me, well...!

Looking at this as a sales scenario makes my actions seem all the more insane. I have a product - me - that I am desperate to sell but I don't believe that anyone would want to buy it. And here was a girl who wanted to buy shares in me. She wanted to buy my product! But I was unable - too screwed up - to sell it to her. How bonkers is that? I never saw her again after that night, funny that...

Buying Signal? What Buying Signal?

Carol would have had to look me straight in the eye and say, "Bryan I really fancy you and want to be your girlfriend. Honest, This is not a wind up. I repeat, this is not a wind-up. Will you go out with me?" before I would have got the message. Duh!

I was notoriously bad at missing the buying signals that I now realise that girls were giving me. Why? Because I didn't believe they were giving them out, so I wasn't looking for them! Yet there they were, right in front of me where I couldn't see them. I'm much better at spotting them now, thanks for asking...

The irony of getting older is of course that you now have the experience that would have enabled you to take advantage of the opportunities that you missed out on when you were young. Trouble is, you no longer get the opportunity! Youth is wasted on the young, it really is...

The Secret to handling Rejection

Now I tell you that story to highlight just how debilitating it can be to mishandle rejection when it comes. For both yourself and others. [Sorry Carol!] The easiest way to handle rejection as a seller is not to experience it in the first place. Guess how do you do that?

Your sales character!

If it's your sales Superhero that does the selling then it's him that will get the rejection not you. If you can do all your selling as your sales character then you can insulate yourself against the toxicity of rejection.

When an actor goes onstage he's simultaneously aware of both the audience and the stage. He knows there are people out there watching him but he's focussed on what is happening on stage. There are two realities co-existing and the actor is part of them both.

Whenever I engaged in the sales process with a prospect, be it on the phone or face to face I did the same thing every time - created a sales character who did the selling for me. That way, if the sale didn't happen then it wasn't me who didn't make the sale, it was my sales character. I nearly never felt rejected or depressed by a bad day. And if you follow my example, then neither will you.

Target Practice

Another benefit of this sales character system is that it'll also help relieve you of the pressure of having to meet targets. Notice I said pressure, not obligation!

Targets suck big time but sadly every seller works to a target that the management set just high enough to mean that the agent will have to push himself if he wants to make bonus. Most sellers are totally unaware of the economics of target setting until they find that they are the one below the line that the client has forced the employer to draw!

In one of the call centres I worked in the target was 8 sales a day. That was 8 sales @ £70 per sale, meaning each agent was expected to bring in £560 of business per day, £2800 per week.

The line hour rate paid by the client was £23 and each agent was paid £6.50 per hour. So for a 7.5 hour day the client paid the centre £172.50 per agent and each agent made £48.75. That leaves a rather healthy £123.75 profit margin per agent, depending on the centre's overheads.

Like most agents, I had good days and bad days. My best day was 17. Now I know that sounds impressive but it wasn't the record. The record for the campaign was 23. Next was someone who started at the same time as me. She got 22 in a day. And so I get the bronze medal with my 17. Hooray! And for the £48.75 I earned that day I brought in business totalling £1,190.00 for the client. Not bad for either of us.

My worst day by contrast was when I started at midday and finished at 8pm. It's 7.45pm and I'm still sitting on a big fat zero. And there is no way that I am finishing on zero. Well, I got that single sale at 7.55pm and I think the entire centre heard my roar of achievement as I made my way to mark it up on the sales board! [The round of applause helped too!]

So the client invests £172.50 per day in me, expecting a £560 return. On a CPA basis - Cost Per Acquisition - that means each £70 sale costs the client £21.56 and for each £1 the client invests they expect it to generate a £3.24 return. So when you crunch the numbers each of my 17 best day sales cost the client £10.14. And of course, my single worst day sale cost the client £172.50!

Pressure? What pressure?

Sink Those SDBs!

Self Destructive Behaviours like the example I gave you earlier can affect you in all sorts of ways, not just drawing up the emotional drawbridge. It could the exact opposite, with you rushing headlong into toxic relationships instead. An SDB is like a sinking ship and you're the last man left on it - you need to jump into the lifeboat quick! It took me years to realise that I had the answer to my SDB problem all the time - adopting a character - but I was never able to make the vital connection until quite late in life. Sometimes our greatest stupidity is thinking that we're clever enough to solve our own problems without outside help. Sales can be incredibly debilitating when you get a bad run without making any progress towards your targets. You begin to question whether you're actually cut out for it at all. And actors suffer from self-doubt just like the rest of you. So what's the answer?

Every SDB has a trigger, an emotionally unpleasant event where you make the wrong choice about how to react. So when that same stimulus happens again, you set up a behaviour loop that eventually becomes a mind trap that's incredibly hard to break out of. But even if you have made a prison for yourself the good news is you can break free! I did, and now you know about adopting a sales character, so can you.

Homework

So now that you can see the advantages of a sales character, write down as many of them as you can think of. Think how many other areas of your life would also benefit from this approach...

COMING UP IN CHAPTER 16...

Bryan takes us into the process of creating a sales character in more depth and shows us how to harness the power twins of imagination and motivation. See you there!

CHAPTER SIXTEEN

WHY ACTORS MAKE THE BEST SELLERS LIST!

Actors make the best Sellers because they have to sell themselves as a product in a competitive marketplace of performers. They can use those same skills to promote whatever show they're in equally effectively. Despite the kudos attached to drama school, it is not a prerequisite for success. Anyone can act but not everyone is an actor, there's no great mystery to it. You're simply pretending to be someone else and you do that already in your own everyday life. So why not use it to help you sell better and sell more!

There are only two kinds of Actor

Character and personality, remember? Ok, so which one are you?

This'll be the foundation of your sales character so it's crucial that you get this decision right. So let's look at your two options:

The Character Option

This is the one where you create someone who looks different to you, sounds different to you, behaves different to you. That's fine for onstage but it can be difficult to pull off if you have to sell face to face.

My team leader in one of the call centres I worked in was delighted when she found out I was an actor. As part of her paperwork she would do a side-by-side monitoring at which she would insist that I do each call in a different accent - Irish, American, Cockney etc. She would be almost wetting herself as the customer said yes and I had to carry on to the close of the call, still doing this accent. This happened several times and I'm not at all sure what the Quality Assurance Department made of it!

The Personality Option

This should really be your preferred option. Someone who is a version of you, looks like you, sounds like you. This will save you from some very funny looks and a possible referral to a psychiatrist that may result from a complete change of appearance, speech and personality!

Whenever I sold face to face I always matched my speech pattern and vocabulary to that of the prospect. This can be tricky and you have to do it subtly enough that your prospect doesn't think you are openly imitating them. If they start to think that, you'll lose them. But when it's done correctly, this acting technique can mean the difference between making the sale and losing it. Why? My potential customers were more likely to buy from me if I came across as being more like them.

How an Actor creates a Character

You start with what is in the script. You know what job he does, where he comes from, what his family life is like, what he does in the script and why he does it. You then have to decide what this person looks and sounds like. Depending on your approach this can be a very quick process or one that takes much longer to come to fruition.

Some actors like to find what they call the 'key' to who the person is. They do this by asking questions that the script doesn't and can't answer. What kind of shoes does he wear? What kind of car does he drive? His favourite colour is what? What does he like on his sandwiches? Does he drink coffee or tea? Does he prefer blondes or brunettes or redheads?

For our purposes, we already know one thing about our sales character. His mission is to sell, that is his purpose in life. He's a Superhero Seller and you are his mild-mannered alter-ego.

Who is your Sales Superhero?

Think for a moment of your favourite hero from whatever genre of fiction you're into. It could be *Star Trek* or *Star Wars*. It could be *Lord of the Rings*, it could be anything. Whatever you're into, who is there in it that could be a template for your hero?

Now try and think of a real-life hero, someone you really admire, maybe a sports star. Football, baseball, boxing, tennis, golf, whatever. Maybe a politician, a former president or prime minister. Perhaps your favourite actor [remember our chapter one exercise?] Again, anyone you really admire and look up to for whatever reason.

Ok, so now you should have two heroes. One real, the other fictional. Ask yourself the kinds of questions actors ask but from a seller's perspective - what do they sell, how do they sell it, how many sales do they make in a day, by how much do they smash their target? What effect do they have on their colleagues? What's their contribution to the team?

Now you have to pick one. Model your sales character on them. It will still be a version of you, but it will be a character you play whenever you are in a sales situation. My advice is to go with the fictional one but it's up to you. Here are a few examples of the kind of thing we are looking for in creating this sales character. Let's imagine that your sales hero character is based on…

James Bond

Imagine Bond was a secret seller instead of a secret agent. How would he go about selling to someone? How would all those gadgets of his from Q Branch come into play? How would he seduce his lady customers into buying his product? If you've ever fancied yourself as James Bond, if you see selling as the art of seduction, then this could be the perfect type of sales character for you.

Sherlock Holmes

On the other hand you may enjoy the intellectual challenge of persuading a customer to buy your product, picking up on those little clues in what they say and how they say it to come to the logical conclusion that this is the perfect product for them!

Hercule Poirot

Or maybe you prefer the whole psychological angle of the business of selling. You want to know what motivates people to do what they do and why they don't want this product that they so obviously need.

Captain Kirk

James Tiberius Kirk never failed to save the day or get the girl, green-skinned or otherwise. He nearly always managed to reason with whatever menace his crew were up against. How do you think he would convince people if he was a seller instead of a starship captain?

Obi-Wan Kenobi

If this guy was a seller he wouldn't stoop so low as to use The Force on a prospect but he would battle against The Dark Side that would seek to stop his prospects from buying his product of their own free will...

Sgt Bilko

Ok I think you get the idea by now...

Of course, the smart ones amongst you will have realised that I chose those examples deliberately. Why? Because, aside from a certain Timelord from the planet Gallifrey in the constellation of Kasterborous known only as 'The Doctor', they are all fictional heroes of mine!

So let me now give you a personal example of a sales character.

Calling Captain Call Centre!

When I first worked as a call centre agent, I discovered that I had a knack for telesales. This was quite surprising as I had always promised myself that the one 'proper job' I would never do was working in a call centre! It seemed to me to be one of the worst jobs in the world and it can be if you're simply doing it, as I was, to pay the bills.

But I'll always be glad I did that job because it was there that I first discovered that I could use my acting skills in the marketplace. Cold calling is not the kind of job that you want to do if you hate having to speak to people you don't know about something you don't believe in.

I had my good days and bad days like everyone else and I had to learn how to deal with the inevitable rudeness and rejection that just goes with the territory. That's when I came up with my first sales character - a sales Superhero, a super seller - Captain Call Centre!

The good Captain was based on several heroes of mine, some of whom I mentioned earlier. He knew more than Bryan did about selling over the phone [OTP Selling, more on that later] and every day I would step into an imaginary phone booth and re-emerge as the Captain.

Just like any other acting performance, I created the character in my head before I began. I imagined how he looked in his Superhero costume without any help from Edna Mole [No capes, dahling!] Obviously he had to sound like me [or did he?] but I didn't have to look like him in the usual Clark Kent alter-ego sense.

Cold calling can be thoroughly depressing if you try and do it yourself - mainly because the quality of training agents are given is so uniformly poor - and a sales character is your best bet for passing the endurance test that working in a call centre can be. If you find work a drag and have yet to work out how to enjoy your job, then creating a sales character like my good friend Captain Call Centre could be the answer you've been looking for!

Creativity Calling!

All human beings are inherently creative. Creation is the process of bringing into existence something that never existed before. [Like your sales character for instance!] Take this book for example, it didn't exist until I wrote it. Think about that. I have created something that never existed before. Every single product in every marketplace was created by someone. For profit. Would you like to be one of those people? Or are you too negative to see the possibilities? I doubt that very much, because otherwise you wouldn't be reading this book, would you?

You are creative too, everyone is. But again, due to humanity's natural negativity too many people fail to realise their creative potential. Please don't allow yourself to be one of them! Be positive on purpose [it's far better for your health, for one thing!] and learn to harness...

The Power of Imagination

Your imagination is a powerhouse of creativity. The ability to imagine is the mechanism of creativity your soul uses via the machinery of your brain. Take this book as an example.

I knew the actual writing of the book would be easy, I've written loads of sketches and scripts and screenplays and songs and articles and copy before. But would I have enough material? Too much as it turns out and a lot of it is going to have to wait for the upcoming training seminars!

If you think about it, really this book is a PSP - a Problem Solving Product. It exists for our mutual benefit. Your benefit is that having invested in the book, you are now discovering that I am helping you to solve your twin problems of how to make more sales and how to handle the risk of rejection that goes with it. And my benefit is that by buying my book you are helping to me solve my problem of how to move from poverty to prosperity! Isn't that a better way to live than running around trying to rip off as many people as possible before you get found out?

So having been given the original idea and making the decision to run with it, aside from the practical issues of what to include and in what order, the most important thing was to make sure that the book met the basic MAN and SAP criteria, which we both know it does. After that it was a simple case of writing and re-writing until I got to the end, which for you is still a few chapters away.

But all the way through that creative writing process I used the power of my imagination to visualise what my shiny new paperback would look like, how it would stand out from the other books on Waterstone's shelf - and how big my name was going to be on the cover! [Just joking with that last one, honest!]

I could see people holding it, looking at it, reading it and buying it. I imagined people ordering it from Amazon, in both the UK and the US.

And perhaps more importantly, I imagined my debts being steadily paid off as more and more people bought the book! That is a very powerful motivator - to know that to be debt-free you only need to sell X books!

COMING UP IN CHAPTER 17...

We get a glimpse into the life of a sales Superhero as we head on over to Talktown and call on Captain Call Centre! See you there!

CHAPTER SEVENTEEN

CALLING CAPTAIN CALL CENTRE!

Whenever I sold over the phone, I always adopted my sales character of Captain Call Centre. Just as Batman had Gotham City and Superman had Metropolis, Captain Call Centre had Talktown. The good citizens of that fair city sold to live and lived to sell. Then came the wicked Master of Mediocrity, always lurking in the shadows, ready to rob the unwary of their selling skills. But Captain Call Centre was only a phone call away, always ready to help those in need to transform their sales technique and turn themselves into a telesales triumph. All he needed was a bestselling sidekick, but who could that be? You maybe?

Character Selling

Okay so it's a little hokey, but this is genuinely what I did when I sold on the phone. I imagined myself as a character and I sold as that character. And it worked. I hit my targets and often beat them. And the time passed more quickly too!

Selling in character in a call centre is a great way to practise this technique as it's less intimidating if you've never consciously tried adopting a persona before. Better to do it over the phone where no-one can see you than try doing it face to face straight away.

A good way to practise is when the phone rings and it's a cold caller. They don't know you so if you do change your voice they won't know you're practising on them. You can pretend to be incredibly posh and hard to impress. You can pretend be incredibly thick and give yourself the perfect excuse to ask them all sorts of questions. If you're feeling particularly cruel you can agree to buy whatever it is and then change your mind. My personal favourite is to tell them that they're not really doing a very good job of selling this thing to me and why don't they try again. Oh the fun you can have with cold callers when you've worked in a call centre yourself!

Cold Calling

If you've never worked in a call centre before then your first time in one of these places can be a bit of a shocker. I've worked in several over the years and there's very little difference in any of them, apart from the quality of the management, or lack thereof. Once you've made your application you will have an initial telephone interview [you can see why they do that] and then you'll either be invited for a face to face interview or an assessment. The latter seems to be the norm now and involves three hours of tedium while you do your routine from *The Apprentice* and try and shine in the midst of the group. Not as easy as it sounds.

Then, once you've got the job you'll find yourself in a classroom of strangers, one or two of whom you may recognise from your earlier assessment group. This is where the disillusionment really starts to set in as the quality of the training you will be given will be so poor as to be non-existent. Too many call centres make the mistake of training their staff in how to make calls but not how to sell. And customer service is no better, believe me.

Who Trains The Trainers?

Your training will be an initial introduction to the company you're employed by and the client you'll be dialling for. There will be the usual 'icebreaker' exercise which is where you'll first think to yourself, "How the hell did he get a job here?" as someone gets embarrassed at having to talk about themselves [not a problem for me!] If someone can't handle a situation as simple as saying hello to someone else, how the hell are they going to sell over the phone?

Truth is, despite the excuses about catchment areas and low wages, call centre recruiters often do a poor job of getting the right kind of person to man the phones. They should employ more out of work actors!

Day two will be spent filling in paperwork for HR and it's only on the third day that you'll get an idea of what it is they actually want you to do. This will be the first time you will have seen the script you'll be working from and, depending on whether your campaign is fully scripted or not, the first thing you need to do is spot which bits are the legalities. Often these are in red on your PC screen and the maxim is, "if it's in red it must be said". Next you look for those points in the script where you can deviate from the text, use your personality and actually sell the thing.

Training will be three days of tedium and then on Thursday you're taken onto the sales floor and buddied up with an 'experienced' agent to see how the job is actually done. This can be a bit of an eye-opener and I've seen people not come back from lunch after being on the floor for the first time. My best piece of advice to a newbie agent was always this:

Take your first call as soon as you can and get it over with. Yes you'll be nervous, yes you'll lose your place on the screen but get it over with. The longer you leave it, the worse it'll be. But if you've got a sales character up your sleeve like I had, it won't be half as intimidating!

Hello, My Name Is...

Bryan and the reason for my call today is to offer you £40 in petrol vouchers as a thank you for trying the rewards and benefits of our new LeisureSaver product. It comes with the first thirty days free and it's all about saving you money on the things you like to do in your spare time. For instance, how often do you like to go to the cinema…?

That was the start of the script for my first selling gig in a call centre. It wasn't the script we were given, that was dreadful. So I changed it to what you've just read. The client liked it and everyone on the campaign ended up using it. Call centre scripts can be the worst things ever to try and read aloud because the people who write them have no idea how to write copy that sells. Too many companies try and do it by themselves [i.e. on the cheap] instead of employing professional copywriters.

As an actor, I'm used to working with scripts and have a good ear for what sounds right when read aloud and what doesn't. Sadly my skills are not those you'll find in many call centre workers, unless they're actors too. So let's take a look at my script again. Read it aloud. Yes you, go on!

Hello, my name is Bryan and the reason for my call today is to offer you £40 in petrol vouchers as a thank you for trying the rewards and benefits of our new LeisureSaver product. It comes with the first thirty days free and it's all about saving you money on the things you like to do in your spare time. For instance, how often do you like to go to the cinema...?

Now you probably spotted the open question at the very end but did you see anything else? Like all the positive words I used? Now let me show you how an actor would lay out a script like this if he were reading it aloud. Spot the difference:

Hello, my name is Bryan

and the reason for my call today

is to offer you £40 in petrol vouchers

as a thank you for trying the rewards and benefits

of our new LeisureSaver product.

It comes with the first thirty days free

and it's all about saving you money

on the things you like to do in your spare time.

For instance, how often do you like to go to the cinema...?

The main advantage of a layout like this is it lets you know where to pause and where to emphasise the end of the line. I used to recite a lot of poetry and a poem-type layout really helps with pacing. Now try reading it again, pausing at the end of each line. In your own time...

See the difference? Now for the last one, this time with the words you should emphasise... emphasised. Read it out again.

> *Hello, my name is **Bryan***
>
> *and the **reason** for my call today*
>
> *is to **offer you £40** in petrol vouchers*
>
> *as a **thank you** for trying the **rewards and benefits***
>
> *of our new **LeisureSaver** product.*
>
> *It comes with the **first thirty days free***
>
> *and it's all about **saving you money***
>
> *on the things you **like to do** in your **spare time**.*
>
> *For instance, **how often** do you **like** to go to the **cinema**...?*

Compare that to the way most sales calls are conducted!

Stay In Character...

...as it's the easiest way to help pass the time. Some centres are stricter on Data Protection controls than others but in general it's a paper-free environment [and whiteboards and their markers seem to vanish into the same alternate dimension as socks!] so your only way of passing the time will be by interacting with those competitors known as your colleagues.

Now I know this can be a drag if you're sat next to Mr Interesting or worse, opposite Mr Foghorn or Little Miss Happy Cackler whose laugh seems to go right through you, but being stuck on a pod filled with numpties for 7 hours a day gives you a great opportunity to practise your acting skills on a captive audience! Time can really drag in a call centre and the breaks are always too short and get scheduled at the wrong times. Spend the time observing the people around you, that's what I used to do. Look for things you can file away for future acting gigs, other characters you can play. Try mimicking their speech patterns and accent - but try doing that one when they're not listening!

Your imagination is really your only means of escape from the cell in which you find yourself entrapped for the rest of the day so you may as well use it fully. We touched on it at the end of the previous chapter so let's look at it again in a bit more detail:

Imagination is...

VISUALISATION - the ability to form an image in your mind of something that does not exist yet or of something that did not happen or has not happened yet.

CREATIVITY - the ability to come up with new ideas for products, new ways of meeting needs and solving problems.

Actors have to use this ability all the time but as a seller you can learn to harness its power too. Remember what I said about being positive on purpose? Well your imagination is the main way you can reprogramme your mind to be positive instead of negative. How?

Before you go into a sales situation, imagine yourself making the sale, picture in your mind the end result you want, the outcome you are after. Keep yourself focussed on your goal, which is making the sale.

And the winner is... You!

Sports psychologists use this tactic with their athletes - before a runner starts a race, he already sees himself crossing the finishing line first. So before the starting gun fires, in his mind he is already at the end of the race and before anybody else. You need to do the same with selling.

Never focus on the journey, only the destination. The destination is the reason you make the journey and your desire to reach the destination is what keeps you going when you encounter obstacles on the way. Think back to that quote from Ed Cole - "Winners are not those who never fail but those who never quit!"

We are all Customers

And we are all PRIAMs too. We all use products and services and the people we are selling our products to only buy them for the perceived MAN or SAP benefits that we, the seller, sold them on. You do the same. That's why you bought this book.

Successful selling is more than just understanding the psychology of the process or having an effective technique to implement that process. It is about knowing what you want to achieve before you even begin, the needs you want to meet, the problems you want to solve and yes, the profit and prosperity you want to enjoy as a result.

It's All A Matter of Motivation

What really matters is your motivation, if your sole motivation is making money then you will be selling yourself short. That is the path that leads to The Dark Side - a shallow, driven, acquisitive lifestyle that will never really satisfy you. And all the time there is the inherent danger that you will degenerate into just another rip-off merchant.

However if your motivation is genuinely to help others [by writing a book, say] in exchange for them helping you [by buying it!] to your mutual benefit, then you are headed for a place of inner satisfaction that will transcend all outward appearances. And be pretty pleasurable and prosperous too, and there's nothing wrong with that.

There's nothing wrong with you having things so long as your things don't have you! Your motive for prospering through selling should always be to meet needs and solve problems, not simply to get money from your customers. That will short-circuit your prosperity potential faster than you can say Bernie Madoff.

By all means get your own needs met first, but when your needs are met remember that the real reason for your wealth is to help others release their own prosperity potential. Inspire them and mentor them to develop the ability to do what you've already done.

What's The Point of It All?

If there is a point to our existence and what we do while we're here then surely it has to be that we leave something behind, not necessarily a memorial or something that testifies that we were here, but something of lasting worth. Something that helps those who come after us to lead better lives than we have. I don't have any children myself but I would hope that every father would want his son to have a better job, a bigger house, a prettier wife and a better life than he did. Every son should be greater than his father. Each generation should make fewer mistakes than the one that went before it. That's the reason why I wrote this book.

Well one of 'em anyway...

[We often joke about the living being entertained by the dead but being captured on celluloid is the closest to immortality many actors will get!]

Homework

Write down everything you can think of about your chosen Superhero sales character template, whether it be James Bond or whoever. How are you going to turn this idea into an actual performance that you can use and do when selling?

Remember, it's not hard and there's no great secret to it. All you're doing is what you used to do when you were a kid - play at being your favourite hero. It's also what you do now in different social situations - pretend to be someone else, a version of you, a better version of you, the ultimate version of you. You are already doing it, which means you know you can do it. So when you sell, why not do it then too!

COMING UP IN CHAPTER 18...

Get ready to start selling as Bryan takes us through the various sales types, selling scenarios and the four stages of a sale. See you there!

Bryan McCormack

CHAPTER EIGHTEEN

OK, LET'S START SELLING!

So enough of the underlying theory, the supportive attitude and the issue of motivation - let's do this thing! This is where we start to get really practical. Having laid a solid foundation we now have to start to build upon it. And that starts right here!

Question - how many different types of sale are there? And what are the different selling skills needed for each one?

Sales Types

OTW - On The Web

PPP - Pitch, Present, Promote

F2F - Face to Face

OTP - Over The Phone

OTW SELLING requires a well laid out website with graphics that are interesting to the eye and benefits-based copy that grabs and holds the reader's attention. This is a passive form of selling as there are no objections the prospect can raise and no means of dealing with them.

PPP SELLING is also passive. It relies on superior presentation skills to grab and hold the viewer's attention long enough to get to the buying stage. This is both the classic market trader's, "Granny Smiffs - free pahnd fur a pahnd!" patter and the more sophisticated approach taken by QVC. [Other shopping channels are available.]

On the other hand, F2F SELLING is entirely interactive and requires you to be reactive to the objections raised by a customer and spot the buying signals they may be giving you.

Similarly OTP SELLING is interactive but is entirely vocal, there are no visual cues to help you interpret the meaning behind the customer's responses. Actors excel at this type of selling for obvious reasons.

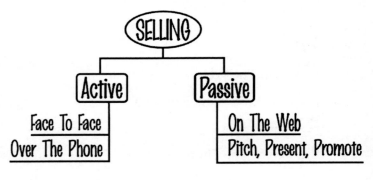

Stages of a Sale

There are all sort of selling books out there, all with different versions of how many stages there are in the sales process. I'm not going to concern myself with the technicalities of the process, there are plenty of excellent resources out there that can already do that job for you. What we are concerned with here is how acting skills can enhance each of the basic elements that make up that process.

Remember how I talked earlier about auditions? They are not just job interviews for actors they are also sales opportunities, an invitation to pitch for the business. So we will be looking at the stages of a sale from the POV of an actor, not a seller.

I will try to keep this as simple as I can and attempt to avoid much of the jargon. But before we get into that, the first thing you need to be aware of is this:

You only get One Chance...

...to make a first impression. If you are selling F2F you need to look the part and everything about your appearance should send a clear signal to your prospect that this is a professional person who knows their stuff. If you want people to get the right impression of you when they first meet you, you need to make sure that everything about you - your clothes, your grooming, your voice - says what you want them to see.

My first impression of you is based on what I see and what I think that says about you, rightly or wrongly. What you then say will cause me to either rethink and redefine my impression of you or reinforce it. So always remember, what they see makes more of an impression than what you say and they see you before they hear you.

OTP Selling on the other hand is an imaginative process. Unlike F2F Selling, the prospect will build up a purely mental picture of what they think you look like based on what you sound like. A good, clear speaking voice, one that is interesting to listen to, is a must for this kind of work, which is why actors like me are so good at it.

Being aware of the need to make a good first impression is a sure sign that you are self-motivated enough to succeed at selling. All your hard prep work will count for nothing if you fall at the first hurdle!

I've got an IDEA!

So here is my simplified actor's version of the sales process:

I - INTRODUCE YOURSELF

D - DEMONSTRATE YOUR PRODUCT

E - ENGAGE THE CUSTOMER

A - ASK FOR THE BUSINESS

This is how an actor approaches the important business of selling himself to a prospective employer. Breaking each section down:

1 - Introduce Yourself

For the fishermen among you, this is where you throw out the hook - how to say hello and make that all-important first impression on the director who may well choose to employ you as a result of what he sees today. This is the actor's equivalent of the initial questioning of a prospect by a seller to find out if he really needs your product or service.

2 - Demonstrate Your Product

This is where you make your pitch, the bit where you actually do some acting. It is where the rubber meets the road and potentially it is the most important two or three minutes of your life. This is the actor's equivalent of a seller displaying his product knowledge, and features and benefits.

3 - Engage The Customer

Having actually acted out whatever bit of script they have sent you, you then sit down and talk to them about your career to date, your experience, where you trained [!], who your agent is etc. This stage is the actor's equivalent of a seller's rapport building and objection handling.

4 - Ask For The Business

The all important seller's stage of closing the sale would come here. For an actor, it is his opportunity to leave a lasting impression when he has gone that will remain with the director. All that is left is for the actor to sit nervously by the telephone for the next few days, waiting for a call from his agent!

And that covers the entire sales process from an actor's point of view!

COMING UP IN CHAPTER 19...

Bryan starts to go through each stage of the process in more detail. We learn about different types of customers and we learn exactly what a SELLER is. See you there!

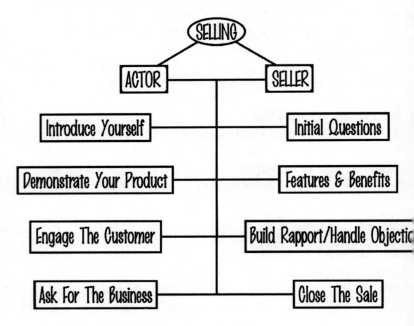

CHAPTER NINETEEN

SELLING YOUR SOUL

So here we are at Stage 1 of the IDEA of Selling. Just to reiterate:

I - INTRODUCE

D - DEMONSTRATE

E - ENGAGE

A - ASK

But before we get started, we need to have our team brief so gather round everybody, budge up that's it, it's ok I don't bite, can you hear me at the back?

Be Prepared!

Before you begin the business of acting, you prepare yourself for what you are about to do - you do some physical limbering up, you do some vocal exercises, some mental exercises to stimulate the 'little grey cells'... before you begin the business of selling you should do the same.

Whatever it is that gets you in 'the zone' to sell - do it! I find music can be a great help, especially dramatic music such as movie soundtracks like those by David Arnold for the recent James Bond movies. It could be Chill Out tracks or even Iron Maiden - whatever works for you, use it!

[And if you are a person of faith, then by all means feel free to pray to your deity of choice and ask him/her/it for help. Rest assured there will be days when you'll need all the help you can get!]

The story is often told of how Laurence Olivier would stand on stage before Curtain Up and tell the audience how lucky they were to be there to see him. Now that story may be apocryphal but if it is true then it is a clear example of what we call focus. An actor must by definition be a self-confident individual to be able to do what he does, even allowing for the occasional attack of stage-fright.

Like a football team huddle before they start the game, develop a routine that gets you focussed on the selling task ahead of you. Ok, so Stage 1.

Stage 1 - Introduce Yourself

At an audition, an actor has to make what we call a big entrance, which unlike those you are used to seeing on TV, is not accompanied by dry ice, a sliding door and a fanfare. ["Aaaand here he is - someone you've never heard of - whoooo's desperate for a job!"] But it has to be equally immediate and engaging without those additional props.

At the introduction stage, the actor knows that from the moment he enters the room, all eyes will be on him. In fact, this is where the auditioning process begins. It does not start when the actor begins to act out the audition piece he has been given. From the moment he walks into the room, it's as if he is on the stage and everything he says and does between the moment he walks in and the moment he leaves is his audition.

The moment your prospect claps eyes on you, you have started your F2F sales process. The moment you say hello to that customer at the end of the phone, you have started your OTP sales process.

Making An Entrance

So the first point of importance for Stage 1 is to understand the power of making a big entrance. And big should not mean completely over the top. Powerful people tend to talk slowly and have a quality of stillness about them that comes from them being secure about their status. People who are desperately trying to be noticed tend to talk quickly and be more manic. Michael Caine was the first actor I remember pointing this out - though not to me personally I'm sorry to say - and when you think about it, it's true isn't it?

I'm not going to patronise you by giving you a whole load of arbitrary rules to follow for making your big entrance, they'll only make you feel self-conscious and uncomfortable. You are a professional, you know what to do. Just be more aware of how important it is to hit the ground running and make that first impression count. If you do not it could cost you the sale before you have even started selling!

Selling Scenarios

OK, so you have your customer in front of you or on the phone. You have just one chance to grab their attention and hold it long enough to get to the next stage. Again, you only have one chance. In an F2F situation you have a combination of verbal and non-verbal cues that you can give your customer, but in an OTP situation it is entirely verbal. We will go through the various selling scenarios you may find yourself in. Even if any of these particular scenarios are not directly applicable to you, read through them anyway. You will still find something you can use in the types of selling situations you find yourself in. OK, so first let's cover F2F.

F2F - Selling Scenario One - The Appointment

Rule one is do not forget the basics. Make sure you allow enough travel time to arrive early for your meeting. Here is a classic example from my favourite sales show, *The Apprentice USA*...

The project manager decided that the team would leave at 10am for a 10.15am meeting. The traffic in any major city at that time of the day would be bad enough, but in New York? They arrived at 10.45am, a full half hour late. And guess what happened? Surprise, surprise - the execs said sorry we have another meeting to go! And served them right. From that moment on, the task was lost, they were destined for the boardroom and everything from there on in was damage limitation.

Always over estimate the amount of time it will take you to get there and if you are early, use the time wisely by having a final rehearsal of your pitch and presentation. When you finally step out of the car, this is like an actor leaving his dressing room, so you should already be in character by this point. Do not try to get into character when you actually meet the prospect, by then it's too late!

So now you are in reception. If you were an actor this would be the equivalent of waiting in the wings, ready to go onstage. Look around you and take in everything you see. The lobby of a company is their first impression maker on their customers. It will also make an impression on you and give you an idea of the kind of people you are dealing with.

See if you can find an ice breaker from anything you see, such as awards or certificates and use that as soon as possible when you introduce yourself to the prospect. This will send a message to the prospect that you are genuinely interested in the company which will help induce favour and shift the balance of power in the forthcoming negotiation. So the door opens and here he comes - showtime!

More basics. Reach out to shake their hand - do it with a firm grip. Nobody likes a limp handshake. A firm grip instantly conveys positive energy from you to the prospect and sends out the message that you mean business. Combine that with looking them straight in the eye and hold their gaze for just a second longer than normal whilst still gripping them in your handshake. This reinforces your positivity and control of the selling situation.

Whatever you say next should be said with a low pitched, steady tone of voice [remember how powerful people speak] and must be said with a smile, the same kind of full on show-us-yer-teeth kind of smile that you will be giving them when they agree to take your stuff!

F2F – Selling Scenario Two – Retail

In this scenario, you are prowling the shop floor, looking for customers who are showing signs of interest in a particular product. The first issue for you is reading their interest correctly - are they giving off buying signals or genuinely just browsing? Next you have to get your timing right and approach them at just the right moment and before any of your so-called 'colleagues' [competitors] beat you to it.

When in retail, I always had my sales character nearby, ready for me to slip into at a moment's notice. A bit like Clark Kent popping into a handy nearby phone booth. Sometimes my mission would be thwarted by some other customer who would intercept me just as I moved in for the kill. This could be really annoying if they were only interested in a £300 cooker when the one you were after was looking at a £1500 widescreen TV. But then sometimes the cooker would sell and the TV wouldn't!

The same principles apply here as with the appointment scenario - make a big entrance, speak slowly and assertively, hold eye contact and find something to make an impression with. The key to this is to match your persona to that of the customer, adapt your speech pattern to theirs, use the same colloquialisms they do, be tactile if they are tactile, serious if they are serious and recognise what kind of customer they are.

What Kind of Customer Are They?

Customers come in four basic types - The Chatterbox, The Geek, The Control Freak and The Novice, although I suppose if you include The Time-Waster [TW] that's five!

THE CHATTERBOX will keep you talking all day if you let them, even after they've bought the thing they came in for. With these customers listening skills are vital since that's what you'll be doing a lot of. Be equally chatty when you do get the chance but once the sale is done and dusted get out of there as quick as you can without making it obvious. This is a potential repeat customer and if you get it right they will come looking for you when they want to buy! Less likely to be a TW.

THE GEEK is into his tech and wants to know all the specs of this PC versus that laptop and is this a 1080P widescreen TV and what is the contrast ratio for this LCD versus that plasma... Make sure your product knowledge is up to scratch with this customer. There is the potential for them to be a TW though so be discerning and cut to the chase if you think there is any possibility that they will not be buying today.

THE CONTROL FREAK is probably the toughest customer to sell to. He knows what he wants and wants to know if you've got it in stock and if it does what he wants it to do and how much is it and when can you deliver and... People like this love to think that they are controlling the agenda and are buying on their terms. If you can let them think that's what they are doing, you are halfway there. Low TW probability - if they are not buying today they will let you know straight off the bat.

THE NOVICE is the most likely to be a TW as they don't really know what they are looking for and what do you recommend and that one looks nice but I really like that one and that's nice too but a bit pricey and that's the same as the one Fred next door's got and well, I dunno…

OTP - Selling Scenario One - Inbound

Customer service is a walk in the park, even when the customer is unhappy at poor service or a wrong delivery or whatever the problem is. You are in a position to make their day by meeting their need or solving their problem by taking their order for the wonderful thing they want to buy from you. And if your boss wants you to upsell at the same time then that's ok too, as they are already in a buying frame of mind.

It's important to keep your voice sounding natural and as if you are interested but be careful not to overdo it - it will come across as false and your customer will pick up on it, trust me. The way to get the balance right is to think of whatever it is that your sales character is into, that way when you speak those positive thoughts will come through in your voice with just the right energy level in your voice to sound genuine.

OTP - Selling Scenario Two - Outbound

Cold calling is probably the hardest job there is, and there are plenty of books out there on the subject. My extensive experience of this could fill a book on its own [note to self - possible sequel] so I'll stick to the main point which is to do with scripts.

Some campaigns will be fully scripted, some will not but an actor will still run rings around anyone else in a call centre when it comes to reading a script from a screen. Why? Actors do more reading of scripts than anything else and we are masters of the art of reading something out without it sounding as if we are reading something out!

Too many call centre agents have poor vocal skills and sadly very few employers take the time and effort to teach skills like these to their staff.

If you are a call centre agent the best thing you can do is to read out loud as often as you can and practice your diction. That does not mean you have to suddenly talk posh - just be yourself but practice will improve the listenability of your voice.

Again, sound enthusiastic and energetic but be professional at all times. Find key words in the script to emphasise, get your manager to print you off a paper copy and if your campaign is not fully scripted, personalise the script to suit your personality. But run it by your manager before you use it with real customers please! And remember whatever is in red must be said! It is red for a reason and that reason is a legal one.

Walking Through An Open Door

This part of Stage 1 would be where the actor introduces himself and has a brief chat with the director about the show and the character he's up for. These initial questions give the director an idea of how much the actor understands what the role entails. And if he likes what he sees and hears he will actually pay attention during the performance!

The seller's equivalent is his initial questioning of the prospect to make sure that he needs the product or service on offer. These questions should always be structured towards the benefits of the product. If you can see that the door to a sale is open - you have established they are likely to be buying today - all you need to do is walk through it and ask them for directions. A sale can be likened to a journey.

The Sales Journey

A Sale is a journey from point of origin to point of departure. Your customer will accompany you on this journey and unless they are a control freak you will be doing the leading as you travel. When customers enter a shop they follow a four point ABCD pattern. They Arrive, they Browse, they Choose, they Depart.

A - Arrive

The customer has come to your shop for a reason. The reason is usually that they want to buy, but not necessarily from you. So you need to establish their intent, their reason for being there. Are they buying today?

B - Browse

If they are looking for a widescreen TV or a PC they will have plenty to choose from. Your job is to narrow down the range of available choices to the one or two that actually meet their need or solve their problem by finding out what features they are looking for, how they will benefit them and how much they are willing to pay for them.

C - Choose

This is where you can lose them if you haven't done your job properly. If they are not fully convinced by what it is, what it does and what it will give them, you will encounter objections. Objections are what you get when you offer a customer something they do not want. Stick to what it is they do want and you will minimise the amount of objections you have to deal with. All the time you are dealing with objections you are not promoting the features and benefits and that is what sells a product.

D - Depart

Never ever neglect this final stage. If first impressions count, then lasting impressions count even more. A happy customer is a potential repeat customer and repeat custom is what you are really after - customer loyalty can mean the difference between marketplace survival and extinction. Make sure you continue to pay attention to them after they have given you their money or signed that credit agreement.

When I sold electricals F2F, the first thing I would do was adopt my sales character. Then I would make the initial connection by reflection [more on this in a moment]. By now the customer has passed point A and we are on to point B. My initial questions would always be based around their available budget and the features they were looking for. My little department was white goods not widescreens and even today I'm still wary when I see a washing machine. But at the same time they give me a warm glow - I regard the very fact that I got a job selling electricals when I am not the least bit technical, as a testament to my skill as an actor!

By the time we have got to point C, I begin to get a feeling for whether or not I am going to get the sale. If it is a couple that are buying, find the one who is more enthusiastic and ally yourself with them to neutralise the negative influence of the one who is not so keen. When it comes to TVs this means you ally yourself with the husband, the wife more often than not will capitulate with a "Well, if that's the one you want..." And when it comes to kitchen appliances it's the other way round! Then it's a simple case of taking the money or setting up the credit agreement and on to point D and ensuring you leave them a lasting impression that means they will be back - and looking to buy again from *you*!

The Economy of Influence

Allied to this initial introduce yourself stage is the power of words. Less really is more and many sellers miss out on a sale because they are too busy talking to listen. If powerful people speak slowly and deliberately, they also never use ten words where three will do. Choose them wisely and try and relate them to the five physical senses, make them as emotive as possible and use them to paint a picture in your customer's mind that links them mentally to the product they want to buy.

It's Not How You Start...

...it's how you finish. [Which is true. We're always more interested in where, how and why someone died than we are in how they got their big break and got started.] In exactly the same way, it's not *what* you say, it's *how* you say it. Here's a simple illustrative exercise:

Think of someone you really find attractive. Got someone? [It's ok if it isn't your current partner, I promise I won't tell, honest!] Good. Now, imagine that person saying these three words to you: "I Love You". Think about how it would be if she/he was to say those three little words to you... ok, that's enough of that....

Now, think of someone you find physically repulsive, someone so completely unattractive that celibacy begins to look like a really engaging lifestyle choice. Now imagine them saying this to you: "I Love You". Aha! Exactly! Yuk, horrible thought, isn't it. But it's the same words, remember! The only difference is who's saying them, how they say them and the context in which they are said.

Same words, two totally different meanings! Words can be thought of as simply empty containers of communication that we fill with meaning. And words have the power to influence. Remember how we talked about your SPI Index? SPI standing for Status, Power and Influence?

Influence is the affect you have on someone else's thinking and resultant actions. The one follows the other. No-one really acts without thinking, your thoughts always precede your actions. The thing is, you think so fast that your mind cannot keep track of all the neural linkages that it fired up to get to the decision that it made that you then acted upon.

Some people can influence others simply by the sheer force of their personality or charisma. The rest of us have to work at it. Emphasise those positive aspects of your personality via your sales character. Don't forget - he is a positive version of you, an extension of who you are in the same way that a golf club is not just a tool in a golfer's hand but an extension of his arm.

Selling in a Buyer's Market...

...is what you do. Your customers can easily go to your competitors and find a similar product or service. Just like an actor, you have to give your customers a reason to buy from you and not the competition and the way you do that is really very simple indeed.

First, realise that it is always a buyer's market - unless your service is bespoke - and second, know what a seller really is. Too many business people I have met fundamentally misunderstand this concept. Those that do understand - which now includes you - will be the ones who remain standing once the economic wind changes, as it inevitably will. Congratulations. So -

What is a SELLER ?

S - SOMEONE
E - ENTHUSIASTIC
L - LOOKING
L - LIKE
E - EVERYONE'S
R - REFLECTION

A seller should be a mirror. That mirror should cast a reflection back to the customer that says I am just like you. And because I am just like you, that means you like me because we always like ourselves more than anyone else, don't we? Of course we do. And because I am like the one person you like the most you want to buy this wonderful thing from me, don't you!

You should never try to make a connection to your customer, you should purposely make a connection by reflection. This simple principle is the reason why the skills of actors like me are so beneficial to sellers like you - they help you to mirror the customer back to themselves. If you can do it convincingly enough, they will buy from you more often and in greater numbers.

People like people like themselves and people like to buy from people like themselves. Why? Because it reinforces the positive aspects of their identity and self-image. You are selling your soul - your mind, will and emotions to your customer as a reflection of themselves. And you are using your sales character to do it.

He is a version of you, an extension of you if you like and you are emphasising those aspects of yourself that match and mirror those of your prospect. You are introducing yourself to the customer as a version of themselves that they can look at via the mirror of your personality. If you can do it well and they like what they see, stand by to sell them not just what they want but whatever you can convince them they need!

COMING UP IN CHAPTER 20...

Bryan takes us through Stage 2, where we learn about features and benefits, demonstrating our product and learn just what SELLING is. See you there!

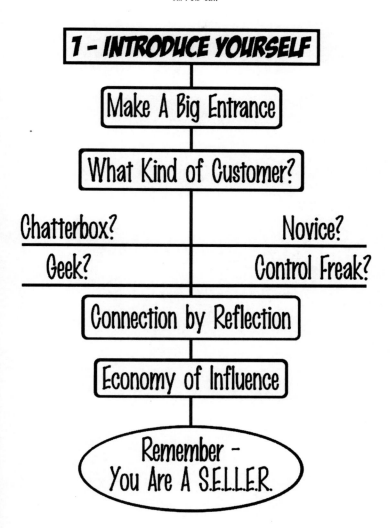

CHAPTER TWENTY

THE ILLUSION OF EXPERTISE

So here we are at Stage 2 of the IDEA of selling. Your sales character has sold his soul to the prospect and got their attention long enough to get them to this stage. Now we need to hold that attention some more and create some interest and intrigue.

Stage 2 – Demonstrate Your Product

This is where the actor would stop talking and start acting. This is where the seller has to match the features and benefits of the product to the customer's needs.

This is where you would start questioning the customer on what it is they want and what they want it to do for them. The questions should always be linked to the benefits of the product. Then you move on to how much meeting that need or solving that problem is worth to them. Unless there is a dirty great piece of PoS [Point of Sale] giving the game away, never ever mention the price until they want to know the price. Then, when you do, it will be easier to overcome a sudden attack of priceitis on the part of the customer. Why? All that time you have spent on the features and benefits is your justification for the price tag.

FAB!

A feature and a benefit are not the same thing. There are benefits to the various features of the product but for now let's keep them separate.

FEATURE - something the product HAS

BENEFIT - something the product DOES

So this widescreen has a higher contrast ratio than this other one, what does that mean? And 1080P and 1080I - what difference does that make?

If this PC has a quad core processor but that one only has a dual core processor, then what do I get for the extra money?

FABs are the reasons why I should buy this product over that one and the reason why I should buy your product instead of your competitors. FABs are why one actor gets cast instead of another.

FABs Are Fab!

Every Actor has FABs and every seller has FABs too. Actors are all lumbered with physical features that they are strongly advised to leave untouched [trout pouts and that one facelift too many are career counter-productive, trust me]. The most successful have capitalised on the genetic lottery and turned their 'look' into an asset.

How talented you are is often less important than how you look. The phrase, "You've got quite an interesting face," is not actually as damaging as it sounds. Whatever you've got about you that's distinctive, use it, capitalise on it, promote it as a feature. If you can do funny voices, if you can sing falsetto, if you can juggle Chihuahuas then that's a feature.

So what are your FABs? What about your sales character, what FABs have they got and how can you capitalise on them? [He's a version of you remember, so you should know the answer to that one!]

From Intro to Demo

In an F2F selling scenario your intro should move seamlessly to your demo with no discernible gap in between. A slick presentation can often sell the thing for you. Take something like a vacuum cleaner for instance. I remember the first time I saw an experienced 'colleague' demo one of these thing. To watch him you would think he had invented it himself. He showed off every attachment, every gizmo and most important of all, he could remove and replace the filter without looking like a chump.

He did not just make the product look like it was easy to use, he looked like an expert with the thing. And that's the way you - sorry your sales character - needs to appear to your customers. I wasn't inspired by that guy to sell loads of vacuum cleaners, but I recognised immediately the powerful effect his apparent expertise had on the customer! [This ability is essential if you want to join the QVC girls! And believe me, it's not as easy as it looks!]

What are Customers?

There's only one way to look at customers. Sometimes they can be a complete pain in the backside but that's usually because they're the wrong kind of customer for what you're selling. Don't get me wrong, I know what poor quality customer service is like just as well as you do, we've all been on the receiving end of it at one time or another. Some of us are guilty of having subjected customers to it just as some customers are also guilty of abusing staff who aren't really the problem but decide to take out their frustrations on them anyway. Despite that though, the customer is often not the enemy, but your thinking about them is.

Customers are the people who are looking after your wealth for you.

Isn't that good? The money you need is in their wallet, money that should rightly be yours. It's calling your name and wants to be yours. In order to release it, you simply have to meet the need or solve the problem of the person who's looking after it for you! That's when the wealth transfer takes place.

Responsibility or Response Ability

You are responsible for yourself. You are responsible for your current level of poverty or your current level of prosperity. If you are in debt, then you are responsible both for getting yourself into it and getting yourself out of it. If you have told a customer their order will be with them tomorrow morning, it is your responsibility to make sure it gets there on time.

[Early in my selling career a lady customer ordered a hairdryer. Being new to the job and a bit of a numpty I forgot to check the stock levels before I took her money and told her it would be waiting for her to collect on whenever day it was she wanted it. And guess what happened? You got it - I ended up buying one with my own money from a nearby branch to avoid looking like a complete twit and having to make a premature career change...]

But you are not responsible for other people's mistakes, only your own. You are not responsible for customers buying things they really can't afford. For one thing you don't have access to their credit report. But that does not absolve you from the responsibility to sell responsibly.

I know of one salesman who, selling PPP to customers in their homes, and having seen the state of the living conditions of one couple, told them that they shouldn't buy his product as they obviously couldn't afford it. He could have used his sales skills to sell his product to them but he responded in the right way - one that maintained his character and integrity, two qualities sadly in short supply nowadays. You will need both if you are to survive and prosper in the modern marketplace. Sellers who are only in it for the money, who are out to fleece as many prospects as possible as quickly as possible will not be the ones who make it in the long run. Why? Because their customers will go to you instead!

You do not have a responsibility you have a response ability! You can respond to the needs, wants and desires of your prospect, solve their product problem for them and turn them into a customer. Your demo should always be flexible enough to respond to your customer's input - remember, acting is as much about reaction as it is about action. The audience can only laugh when you stop speaking after the punch line!

[Two ears, one mouth - so listen twice as much as you talk!]

The Main, er, Features of the Benefits are, er...

Product knowledge is vital to your success, but you should always look at the product from the customer's point of view. It's easy to get geeky with all the various doodads that this thing has and does, but they count for diddlysquat if they are not relevant to the question of is this a MAN product or a SAP product?

There is nothing more embarrassing than being asked a question you don't know the answer to. Except perhaps one of your 'colleagues' butting in to correct you!

In an OTP selling scenario though you need to question effectively to highlight the FABs that are really relevant. For instance, I used to sell a product that gave the customer discounts on various leisure activities. So my first job, having introduced myself, was to get them interested in the idea of saving money doing the things they enjoy. Harder than it sounds, believe you me.

So Mr Smith, how often do you like to go to the cinema? Not as often as you would like? Well with This Wonderful Thing we can help you go more often because we can save you...

Practice, practice, practice!

We have all heard the catchphrases - Practice Makes Perfect, Preparation Prevents Pathetic Performance etc, but if there is one thing that sets successful sellers apart from the rest of the pack it's the fact that they are constantly looking for ways to improve. Like buying a book on acting skills as selling tools for instance!

We all need to practice to keep our skills up to date and sharpen our reflexes, Actors as much as sellers. Where do you think the military would be if they didn't constantly practice and prepare? Dead, that's where they'd be and unless you want to kill your career as a seller then don't be so arrogant as to think that you don't need to practice too. The minute you think you've made it is the minute when you start to lose ground. And it'll probably happen so slowly that you won't realise it until it's too late. Then you'll start trying to grab onto what's left but the harder you try to hold on the faster it slips through your fingers.

Never forget, inflexibility is the foundation of failure.

But you're not going to fail are you? No, you're going to maximise your potential by actually doing what I'm telling you to do. You are going to take what works for me and make it work for you. You are going to be The Best Seller You Can Be aren't you? Of course you are!

And I'm not finished helping you yet, so let's just remind ourselves why we are doing all this.

What is SELLING?

So far we've defined what an ACTOR is and what ACTING is. We've also defined what a SELLER is. So now let's complete the set by defining what SELLING is:

S - SINCERE
E - ENGAGEMENT
L - LOOKING
L - LIKE YOU'RE
I - INTERESTED IN
N - NEEDS NOT
G - GAIN

Good, isn't it!

The bottom line is that you are looking to persuade people to part with their cash and give it to you in exchange for this wonderful thing that you have [like a book!]. But you must appear more interested in the person that you're selling to than you are in the sale you're looking for from them. Nowadays most folk are quite savvy about selling, which means sellers will have to raise their game.

But even when we know we're being sold to, we often don't mind if the person doing the selling makes us feel good about either the thing he's looking to get us to buy or ourselves. An actor's main job is to entertain and make an audience happy that they've just watched something they enjoyed. [Most criticism of actors is nothing more than prejudice because the actor in question doesn't do the one essential thing that is the subject of the next chapter.]

In the same way, a seller should aim to make the experience of being sold to entertaining in that it should be enjoyable. A nice friendly person who's looking to help solve your problem and some good chat, makes for a better chance of a sale. Why? Because people are led by how they feel rather than what they think. People are mostly emotional not rational, and that includes the men!

If you - if your sales character - can get your prospect to feel good about parting with their cash in exchange for your Wonderful Thing, then not only are they more likely to do so, they're more likely to come back and do it again! Repeat business is what you're after, remember.

See The Sale Before You Sell

This is a really important principle that applies to every kind of goal setting imaginable. As an actor, the ability to use your imagination and visualise a realistic unreality - the fictional world of the play or movie - is essential. Everyone has this ability yet few people use it effectively in their everyday life, and that includes most sellers.

When you visualise something, all you're doing is reinforcing your self-belief in the likelihood of it happening. Actors use this ability all the time when they rehearse and nowadays with the amount of green-screen work actors have to do, it's more vital than ever.

Have you never rehearsed something very important that you want to say to someone? Of course you have! Ok, so what happens in your mind when you're saying the words? You can see them, you can picture where and when it's gonna happen, how they'll respond, how you'll feel. Do the same with your sales!

COMING UP IN CHAPTER 21...

Next up is Stage 3 where Bryan takes us through handling objections and we discover the secret to RAPPORT. See you there!

2 - DEMONSTRATE YOUR PRODUCT

THE ILLUSION OF EXPERTISE

See The Sale Before You Sell

Features	Benefits
Cost	Quality
Responsibility	Response Ability

Remember What You're Really SELLING

CHAPTER TWENTY ONE

REAL MEN BUILD RAPPORT

So here we are at Stage 3 of the IDEA of selling. Your sales character has matched the features and benefits of the product to the customer's needs. Now it is time for -

Stage 3 - Engage The Customer

This is where the actor would talk about his experience and career and try to convince the director that he should be the one that gets cast. For the seller, this is where the process of rapport building comes into play, as well as objection handling. More sales are lost here than anywhere else, so it is vital that you understand the importance of this stage.

Rapport and objection handling are the selling equivalent of an accident blackspot. No matter how many signs the highway department put up warning drivers to slow down, they still get caught out.

When I was a call centre team leader, part of my job was listening to, and scoring, agent's calls according to the client's criteria. I was forever telling agents that they could have made more of this or that, depending on what the customer had said during the call. There aren't really that many things a potential customer can do during this process:

1. They can either say yes or no.

2. They can ask a question [What does it do?]

3. They can raise an objection [It's too expensive!]

4. They can give you something you didn't ask for.

Which brings me to my next point:

Free Information! Who Wants It?

You receive millions of pieces of information every day and filter them according to their importance, relevance and interest to you and your worldview. Ever had the wife trying to talk to you when you're trying to watch something really interesting on the telly? [And getting in a huff because what's on the telly is obviously more important than what she's saying? Been there, mate, believe me.]

Your customers do exactly what I've been doing throughout this book - giving you free information about their favourite subject - themselves!

Here's a little project for you - once you've finished the book, go back and see how much free information I've given you about myself. Write down everything that you think helps paint a picture of the kind of person I am. Then think how you would sell your product to me...

Any time a prospect gives you some free information, pounce on it like a cat on a mouse. Even if it's something that you find incredibly tedious - like say fishing or caravanning - or something you find utterly repulsive - like say pre-school children or dinner parties

- you must take that free information and feed it back to them in a way that makes them believe that you are as interested in it as they are.

Alternatively you can take the opposite tack, play the dunce card and question them on it, "Train spotting? Wow that sounds interesting! How did you get into that?" Treat them like they're an expert on the whole subject. Even if they're not really their ego will be flattered that they have someone to show off to. If you can manage the free information that your that customers give you correctly, this will help you to deal with the problem of objections and how to handle them.

Operation Objection

Objections are statements made by customers that are in opposition to what you are trying to achieve - a sale. They are the reasons why the customer thinks that what you're offering isn't the MAN or SAP product that you think it is. Sales people often talk about isolating objections or finding the real objection, which isn't always the price!

I once heard the great Brian Tracy say that objections are what you get when you stop talking about what the customer wants, which is brilliant.

Trouble is, too many companies neglect teaching their staff how to do that. In fact, in almost every selling job I've ever had, I've encountered the same basic problem which is that at no time did the people training us spend any time teaching us how to actually sell! In general, there is far too much emphasis on PK [Product Knowledge] and not enough on SS [Selling Skills].

As an actor, objections are what you get when you fail to engage with the audience. There are a lot of after-dinner speakers who have misjudged the mood of their audience and fallen flat on their inflexible faces. As a seller, if you fail to engage with your audience on their level, you will encounter objections, guaranteed.

Think back to your four customer types - what sort of objections do you think they are likely to come up with? What sort of objections have you run up against yourself? At what stage of the sales process did they appear?

It always helped me to think of dealing with objections as being a bit like an SAS operation and too many sellers come a cropper because they haven't done their homework in preparation for their next encounter with the enemy. Like any military campaign, you first gain an insight into your enemy's motivations, put yourself in his place and then plan for success using an attack strategy he will not be expecting. Easy really...

Remember this, your sales character is a version of you that is a more successful seller than you are. He knows how to relate to people where they are, he understands their motives and the kind of lives they lead. If you're not a people person, then you will find sales tough going. You must be genuinely interested in people, or alternatively be highly skilled at appearing to be interested in people. Convincibility is the other key ingredient to a successful con trick [aside from appealing to people's greed or vanity] and if you've ever been hustled by a con-man you will know how effective a skill this can be!

Real Men Build Rapport

The key concept behind rapport is mutuality or common interests. People like people like themselves. Why? Because they reflect and reinforce their self-image. And because that's true it's a fact that people like to buy from people like themselves. It's an actor's job to portray people that his audience can either identify with if he's a hero or enjoy hating if he's a villain. Either way, acting is all about using your personality to create an extension of yourself that people can relate to.

Rapport is linked to the concept of favour which we'll look at in a moment. But all I really want to say on the subject is this - sellers all too often fail to build rapport because they aren't interested enough in the customer. Rapport is a bit like sympathetic resonance, which all the musicians among you know about. A tuning fork will set off another tuning fork. Everything vibrates at a particular frequency and if an actor can find the frequency of his audience, he can get them to vibrate! So with that in mind, let's look at the two schools of thought on the subject of rapport and favour:

Rapport v Favour

The first school of thought is that you build rapport to gain favour. Favour is a bit like having the biggest kid in the playground on your side, and if anybody wants to have a go at you, they need to deal with him. Favour is when doors open for you that stay closed to everybody else. Why? Well it's usually because the person you have favour with really likes you.

Favour v Rapport

The second school of thought is that you gain favour to enable you to build rapport. This involves making a deposit in your goodwill pension account but the trouble is that this can make people suspicious of your motives. If someone is suddenly nice to us for no apparent reason, our instinctive reaction is, "What's he after?"

Personally I subscribe to the first one - you build rapport, thus enabling you to gain favour, thereby potentially opening doors for you. Favour is the invisible man who can move unseen to get things done on your behalf. But you need to work with him, not against him, and always remembering of course to get your timing right, make the most of your connections and take advantage of the opportunities that come your way!

The RAPPORT Method

Let me save you the effort of sticking 'rapport' into Google and wading through the thousands of results you'd get - the best definition I have ever heard came, I think, from a guy named Lance Wallnau. I've never forgotten it and it's a cracker! Here it is, ready?

R - REALLY
A - ALL
P - PEOPLE
P - PREFER
O - OTHERS WHO
R - REFLECT
T - THEMSELVES

Isn't that great? And it's exactly what an actor does too!

If you can change the way you speak and moderate your vocabulary and vocal style to mirror those of your prospect, then you are much more likely to win them over and turn them into a customer. This is the key to working with and winning over connections - customers for your talent. Reflect them back to themselves. How hard can that be?

Rapport is nearly always talked about as something that you build, with the inherent implication that it takes time. The best statement I've ever heard made about building rapport came from my mate Rintu: assume you already have it!

This is exactly what an actor does when he goes onstage: if he didn't have complete self-confidence and belief in what he was about to do he would never go out there [especially to do panto!]

An actor spends all his time trying to get into other people's heads and understand how they think. Rapport is simply two minds that think along similar, parallel lines, like train tracks. As a seller you need to be able to understand what makes your prospect tick and reflect that back to them through your conversational skills and body language.

Actors always look at a scene they are about to play from three different angles - their own character, the other character and the audience. Try looking at your own sales scenarios from someone else's perspective - your customer's for instance. Or if you're really feeling brave, get your manager or more experienced colleague to observe you and give you some feedback. That last one's not for the fainthearted but you do still want to be The Best Seller You Can Be don't you?

Perception Is Everything

What I'm talking about here is usually called perceptual positions, which is just a fancy name for seeing the same thing - a scene in a play or a sales scenario - from three different viewpoints. You've probably heard it said that perception is reality, which is true. [Remember what I said earlier about Rabbie Burns?] If you believe in God, for instance, then your behaviour - which is based on your beliefs, values and attitudes - will reflect what you believe. Everything in your world will be viewed in relation to that belief, whereas your humanist counterpart will do the self same thing with what he believes. You will both live in different worlds.

If you are serious about seeing how you really appear to the rest of the world your best bet is to get your camcorder and film yourself. Don't try and perform for the camera, the point of the exercise is to see you as you really are. [Keep your sales character tucked away for the moment, you can practice with him later.] People are always self-conscious when the TV cameras are around and what you see on reality shows are people who have got used to the cameras being around and have relaxed a bit.

So, there are two ways of going about this. The first is to switch the camcorder on and leave it running in the corner of the room. Just go about your normal activities and try to ignore it. You want to film yourself coming into a room, maybe the kitchen, and doing something ordinary like making a cuppa. What you're looking for is how you move, the way you hold yourself. And don't suck your tummy in, that's just going to defeat the object of the exercise. [You can do that when you do the whole naked-in-front-of-the-full-length-mirror bit later.]

I guarantee that you will be shocked by what you see. It's a natural reaction - and one that I've personally experienced - to think, "Oh my God, do I really look like that?" Don't worry, you're not alone. I can remember the first time I appeared on telly as myself and it's amazing the things you see yourself do that you were previously blissfully unaware of. But now there they are, laid bare in front of your own eyes. But keep remembering, this is the you that everyone else sees so you absolutely owe it to yourself to check out what it is that you present to the rest of us as your product. Rest assured there is huge room for improvement in both your presentation and marketing strategy!

Me, Myself & I

The second way of doing it is to film yourself talking. Again there are several ways you can do this. You can have an imaginary conversation with an unseen person, go through a mock interview [use some questions from one of the celebrity interviews in the Sunday papers, the kind where they print the questions and responses] or better still just talk about your favourite whatever - sport, football team, TV show, person, event etc.

The good thing about this is that you get to hear what your voice really sounds like to the rest of us. Actors are more aware than anyone of the power of the human voice and the use of inflection and intonation. Most people tend to use very little vocal variation and as a result sadly have voices that are not really that great to listen to. I'm sure you can think of several examples from your own social circle. An uninteresting voice is hard to listen to and less likely to say anything that sticks around in your memory - which is why so many presentations are an endurance test.

In addition, the sound of the voice you hear coming out of your mouth when you speak is affected by the vibrations of the bones in your skull and the shape of your throat and your nasal cavity. This is why I can almost guarantee that you will get a shock when you hear yourself for the first time like we do! And yes, I've been there too.

But remember this is a good thing - unless you are fully aware of what the rest of us see and hear you will remain ignorant of where you are falling down in the presentation of your core product - you! And this is where the real fun begins. You can now start to experiment with ways to improve on what you've discovered - all your previously unknown presentational deficiencies. Mess about and do all that performance stuff I advised you not to do at first, do silly voices and ponce about making a complete prat of yourself, do as much air guitar as you like but above all have some fun finding ways to look and sound better than you do now.

When I watched me as myself on telly I found there were all sorts of little mannerisms that I never knew I had. Nothing major but little things that made me think, "I don't do that do I? Oh God, I do! Why do I do that? Blimey, better knock that on the head pretty sharpish!" And so I went and did exactly what I advise you to do, become more self-aware [which isn't the same as being self-conscious] and do all you can to make the most of yourself, the self that the rest of us - and that includes your customers - see every day. You won't regret it I promise you!

Homework

You haven't had any homework for a while, so aside from the worthy camcordering exercise above you should work on your rapport skills. It's something you've been doing socially already - now do it on purpose!

Start with someone you know that you don't really get on with that well but would like to. Find out as much as you can about them from all the free information they give you and use that to build some rapport, always remembering to visualise the result before you begin. Then move on to someone you know that you don't really get on with but need to and do the same thing again. Remember - the purpose of rapport is favour!

COMING UP IN CHAPTER 22...

We're nearly there now - only one more stage to go! Bryan guides us through the tricky business of closing the sale! See you there!

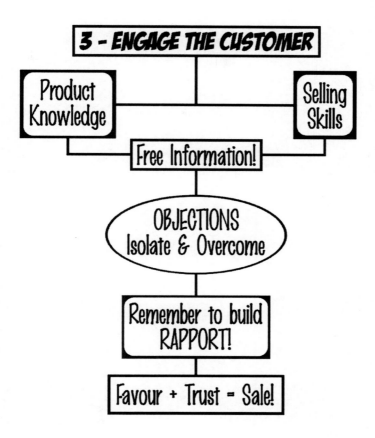

Bryan McCormack

CHAPTER TWENTY TWO

DEAL OR NO DEAL?

So here we are at Stage 4 - the final stage of the IDEA of Selling. This is the single most talked about aspect of selling and it always puzzles me why. If you've gone through the previous three stages correctly then this last one should either be a doddle or at least less difficult than before.

Stage 4 - Ask For The Business

This is where an actor would do all that he could to leave a lasting impression. The acting bit of the audition is over and it's where the director or producer will chat to the actor to see if they click. The person doing the auditioning has two things running through his head:

1. Is this the right person for the part? Do they look right, sound right? What will they add to the mix? Are they a good contrast to the actors I've already cast? Will they make my project better by being in it?

2. Do I like them? Can I see myself getting on with this person for the next however many months or weeks it is? Do they have an ego the size of Mount Rushmore? And if they do, is it worth the hassle?

The poor actor is frantically trying to gauge which of these are going on in the director's head and winging it with his answers to the questions that come his way.

Above all he must try and establish some sort of connection, say or do something, anything memorable [within reason] that will maintain his position on the list of 'possibles' when his next competitor follows him. Nowadays of course, casting directors do a lot of this kind of thing instead but an actor must still give reasons why he should be the one that gets picked over anyone else.

When I worked for a certain leading UK supermarket I once went for a stock control job interview at another branch that was nearer to my home. The interview went really well but I lost out to someone less experienced who worked in that branch that the interviewer knew better. Her exact words were, "I don't know why I'm giving him the job but I just think he's got that extra something..." Similarly, as a seller, you need to have that, 'certain something' and give your customer enough reasons to say yes and pick you and not the opposition. Just be sure you've got 'em hooked before you try to reel 'em in!

You know you want it...

Closing a sale is just like doing comedy and asking someone out - timing is everything! And as Brian Tracy points out, when you get the timing wrong, you kill the sale! Now I'm not going to spend time going over sales closing in detail as there are plenty of specialist books on this subject which I'm sure you've already read. I take a very simple approach to this whole area.

There are only two people who can close the sale - you or the prospect. To close a sale you need to match up your desire to help them get the stuff with their desire to own the stuff. If both parties feel that everybody wins, then a sale is a dead cert. You want them to buy, they want to buy, so go help 'em buy! Winners want others to win too.

Selling is all about getting your prospect to the place where you can get a positive close, not a negative one. There will be a close, your job is to make sure it's the right one for both of you! Without a close, there is no sale and closing is all about communication. It's mostly a verbal skill and whether you have a talent for it or whether it's an ability that you pick up along the way, closing a sale is all about words.

Go on!

People are visual, not verbal and words paint pictures in people's minds. Choose the right words and you'll get a Rembrandt, use the wrong ones and you'll get a Jackson Pollock!

You've probably lost count of the number of times you've chatted up a girl in a pub. Think back - how carefully did you choose what you said? How hard did you think about what to say? How much attention did you pay to her reaction to what you said? And how hard did you then think of a way to say what you really wanted to say and say it at just the right time? Well, dealing with customers is exactly the same - in effect you need to 'chat them up'! And chatting up girls is as much about them as it is about you, if not more so.

Remember what I said earlier about opportunities? They are temporary times of optimum advantage dues to favourable conditions. Chatting up a girl is pointless unless you can get the conversation to the place where you actually ask her out [and convince her - give her enough reasons - to say yes!] Closing a sale is exactly the same.

Becoming A People Person

Actors spend all their time observing the people around them, building up a mental portfolio of different personality types that they can use to build characters with. Personally, I used to walk about with a little notebook and write down any gestures people made that interested me, like the different ways they hold newspapers. [Railway stations are great places for people-watching, due to all the hanging around that people do there. Airports can be even better!] I'd note down how people walked, their expressions and especially their voices, speech patterns and any snatches of overheard dialogue.

Body language as it's called is an essential weapon in an actor's arsenal of character-making. But more important is his ability to discern different types of people. As a seller, you need to be able to discern different personality types too so when you 'chat them up' during your sales scenario, your sales character will know the kind of person he's dealing with and adjust his approach to the sale accordingly.

Up On The Downs

They say the world is split into extroverts and introverts. I'm not sure I'm entirely convinced by that as people are usually a mixture of the two, depending on their mood and the social situations they find themselves in. Actors most certainly are extroverts but as I pointed out earlier, even we like to step out of the limelight for a breather every now and then. Being the focus of attention all the time can be very wearing, believe me. But as a pure generalisation yes, there are people who always seem to be on the up escalator of life and others who make you want to run a mile - the kind of people who can darken a room just by entering it!

Whenever you engage a prospect, they can only make one of three responses - positive, neutral or negative. Neutral responses are the worst as they give you so little to go on [which is why open questions are so useful]. Extroverts tend to self-aware, though obviously their ego does have a habit of getting just a teensy-weensy bit in the way! Introverts on the other hand, tend to be self-critical, and equally critical of others, if not more so! So learn to discern the kind of person you're dealing with.

Of course, your sales character will have been doing this throughout the sales scenario, not just at Stage 3 [Engage The Customer]. Won't he? Yes Bryan, I can hear you cry, he will...

Oh, just buy the **** thing!

But if it doesn't work out then don't let frustration get the better of you. Some people will jump ship at the last minute and despite what they say you cannot make anyone do anything you want. People still have free will and you can never get so inside their head that you know everything that's going on in there. But the more you can see things from their point of view, the more likely you are to triumph.

If you want to be negative then remember that the deceiver can also be deceived. Not getting the sale is not the important thing, what's really important is what you learn from that sale scenario that you can add to your collection of tools for detecting time-wasters!

And never allow yourself to set up an SDB in your head just because things didn't work out - they were simply the wrong customer for your product. Use the experience to better learn how to detect the right ones!

Selling In A Nutshell

It's all about the relationship you have with the prospect, that's what turns them into a customer. It's more important than whatever it is you're selling and it's how you convert selling into buying. It's when the way you sell and the way they buy mesh together that's when you get results. It's when you can convince them that you can satisfy their need with what you've got. It's when they are sure that you are genuinely interested in them, that you have something in common. It's when you, as a professional persuader, make things happen instead of waiting for them to happen! It's when you follow your instincts and motivate yourself to become progressively more and more like The Best Seller You Can Be.

And that person is your sales character.

COMING UP IN CHAPTER 23...

Bryan shows us how to put all this together and takes us to the best place he knows - yup it's back to the girls [and boys] at QVC!

4 - ASK FOR THE BUSINESS

Leave A Lasting Impression | Get Your Timing Right

Observe Buying Signals | Chat Them Up!

Who Will Close?

YOU? — THEM?

SALE!

248

CHAPTER TWENTY THREE

TELLY SALES

The best example we have of acting and selling working together is QVC. Currently based at Marco Polo House in Wandsworth in London, the channel launched on Sky in October 1993.

Quality, Value, Convenience

Now if you're anything like me, you'll have a real love/hate relationship with QVC. I've lost count of the number of notebooks I've filled with reams of product numbers. If you were to tot up all the things you would buy if money was no object, then in your head you could easily spend squillions of pounds. Aside from not watching at all, the safest bet is probably to watch with the sound off! [Or use your Sky Plus like I do, purely in the name of research of course…]

Like almost everything in modern British culture, and no, that's not necessarily a criticism, QVC started in the United States. Based in West Chester in Pennsylvania, since 1986 they have been broadcasting 364 days a year to an estimated US audience of 90 million. Here in good old Blighty it's more like 6 million. In the US they shift product worth some 7 Billion [with a B] dollars and in the UK about 350 Million [with a measly M] quid.

There's QVC Germany and QVC Japan and there are plans for QVC Italy too. As well as the website there's the interactive service on satellite, their Facebook page and you can even shop with them on your mobile! And there's a heck of a lot of shopping being done - it's reckoned that one in five homes in the UK have bought something from QVC. And when you learn that in a year they shift something like 14 million items here, and when you work out that that's about 40,000 products a day you realise that these are sellers who know what they're doing!

Homework

Remember your first lot of homework way back at the end of chapter one? Well here's your last lot and possibly the one you'll gain the most from as we approach the end of our time together [It's been fun, hasn't it!] Go back and watch the channel again and make another set of notes.

But this time I want you to pay particular attention to anything and everything that you notice the presenter doing that reminds you of something I've pointed out to you in this book. Then I want you to compare this set of notes with the first ones you made and see just how much more you've noticed second time around!

Your Host For This Hour...

The really interesting thing for me is how many actors and performers there are amongst the channel's current slate of presenters. That should tell you something about the practical application of what I've been sharing with you in this book. Of the 23 presenters listed on the website at the start of 2010, how many actors/performers do you think there are?

Ok, I'll save you the trouble of checking - there are 13 of them. That's more than half - even my maths is good enough to work that one out!

Now I admit this next bit is a bit hokey but if there's 23 of them and they shift £350M that works out at £15M each! How would you like to be responsible for fifteen million quid's worth of sales in a year! Yeehah!

So when you do your final homework exercise try, if you can, to watch an hour fronted by The Queen Bee of QVC herself...

Julia Roberts [No, Not That One!]

...as she's the lady that you can learn the most from. Ju has been with the channel since the very beginning. Think of how many different products she must have sold in that time. Think about how good at both selling and presenting she must be to still be at it 16 years later! She should have written this book really but she was busy so...

Although Googling her does, unsurprisingly, produce lots of screengrabs of her boobs, if you look at her biography you'll see that, like most TV people, her life went through a series of TTC stages before she found her true vocation. Having started as a cabaret dancer, she then did acting bit-parts and got into presenting in 1989 at the London Motorshow.

The story goes that it was a tape of this performance that she sent to her local cable company in Croydon, and on the strength of it they gave her a job. The experience she gained there meant she was perfectly positioned to take advantage of the opportunity afforded by a certain new shopping channel... [Remember folks, T+T+C =O!]

I'm sure Ju had little idea when she did that first bit of presenting at that Motorshow in 1989, that in just 4 years it would indirectly lead to the QVC gig. This is a woman who knows more about selling on TV than anyone else in the UK and I can assure you, what she and her colleagues do is not easy at all. The trick is to make it look easy...

As well as Ju, try and catch this bloke:

Paul Lavers

When I first saw Paul on QVC I recognised him from his appearance in *Doctor Who*. He appeared as Swordsman Farrah in the 1978 Tom Baker story, *The Androids of Tara*, fact fans. [Now here's a funny thing - I can recognise actors who've been in Doctor Who when they're in other TV shows, but not the other way round. Funny that...]

Paul was with QVC for its first six years [1993-99] and is now with The Entrepreneur Channel, Sky 682 at the time of writing.

His Spotlight entry describes his voice as "Friendly and Melodious" and if you listen to him you can see why. Vocal skills are vitally important to sellers and you can learn a lot about how to effectively use your voice from watching an actor and presenter like Paul. As well as...

The Chorus Line

...who comprise the 12 other current presenters who are either actors or performers of one kind or another. Head on over to the website sometime and check out this lot and some of the things they did prior to QVC:

Julian Ballantyne, Simon Biagi, Charlie Brook,

Debbie Flint, Jill Franks, Dale Franklin,

Pipa Gordon, Debbie Greenwood, Jilly Halliday,

Anthony Heywood, Alison Keenan, Claire Sutton

In amongst that lot you'll find skills in dancing, singing, modelling, journalism, TV and Radio production, voice-over artists as well as several decades worth of accumulated experience in all sorts of other TV and Radio presenting. That's quite a combined skill set to have at your collective disposal...

Why You Should Buy This Wonderful Thing

Selling on the telly isn't easy as those hopefuls who went along to the channel's 2006 "Search For A Presenter" open roadshow audition can no doubt testify. And before you ask, no, I wasn't one of 'em. I've been to enough auditions in my time to know what to expect and thought I'd give the rest of you a chance to see what it's like!

The webpage stated that hopefuls didn't need previous professional presenting experience just, "loads of enthusiasm and a personality that our viewers can connect with". Sound familiar?

If there is such a thing as an official QVC Selling Style I'd hazard that it's all about being honest, seeming genuinely interested in the people you're selling to, using your voice correctly and doing all you can to establish a connection with potential customers using a version of your own personality known as your sales character.

If you're feeling particularly brave then get your camcorder out again - and no, this isn't homework - and film yourself as if you were on the channel flogging something. It could be something fairly easy like your mobile phone but I guarantee you that, whatever you choose, you will run out of things to say about it quicker than you think.

Then you can go back and watch Ju [and the rest of them] doing it properly with a new appreciation for just how hard a job like hers really is. Not everyone can do it and even fewer can do it well. See? I told you acting and selling had more in common than you thought…

COMING UP IN CHAPTER 24...

It's almost time for Bryan to say goodbye as we reach the end of the book and The Final Chapter. All together now - Aaaw… See you there! [Sniff!]

CHAPTER TWENTY FOUR

THE FINAL CHAPTER!

Well here we are, 24 chapters later and we've reached the end of our journey into the twin worlds of acting and selling. Which is, of course, not true at all as we both know that the journey has just begun!

You are now equipped with pretty much everything you need to start using your new found skills to improve your selling. In this book I've given you most - but not all - of what I know about using acting skills as selling tools. These are lessons I've learned the hard way on the front line of both acting and selling. Just think of all the time, effort and energy I've just saved you, grab that advantage with both hands and go for it!

So here is my last word on acting:

Ricardo Montalban

Okay, so that's two words, but what the heck. The star of 1970s hit TV show *Fantasy Island* and the movie, *Star Trek II - The Wrath Of Khan*, he summed up an actor's career like this:

- First they say "Who is Ricardo Montalban?"
- Then they say "Get me Ricardo Montalban!"
- Then they say "Get me A Young Ricardo Montalban"
- Then they say "Get me A Ricardo Montalban Type"
- Then they say "Who is Ricardo Montalban?"

That's an actor's life in a nutshell and I've never forgotten it. Some are lucky enough, no that's not true, some have enough residual affection from their first time in the spotlight to give them the opportunity for a second. It's never on the same scale as their initial success but it can be more rewarding. Take the actor Tom Baker, who, in the second half of his career, is now employed almost exclusively by adults who watched him as children. It can happen. For most actors though, once the spotlight moves on, it returns us to the darkness of obscurity from whence we came. The best we can hope for is that we get to be remembered for a bit longer than we thought we would be...

Ok, so let's finish up by summarising all the good stuff that you've learned in Act Two.

- Sell your soul
- Negativity comes naturally, so be positive on purpose
- There are seven spheres to your life
- There's an advantage in being an everyman
- Nobody else can sell like you do
- Sell yourself like you would sell yourself
- Remember the Universality Factor
- Status, Power and Influence - What's your SPI index?
- Grow into your goals and be specific
- Live your life inside out
- Sink those SDBs!
- Who is your sales Superhero?
- The IDEA of selling:

- o I - Introduce
- o D - Demonstrate
- o E - Engage
- o A - Ask
- Learn the economy of influence
- FABs are fab!
- You have a response ability not a responsibility
- See the sale before you sell
- What is a SELLER ?
  - o Someone
  - o Enthusiastic
  - o Looking
  - o Like
  - o Everyone's
  - o Reflection
- Free information! Who wants it?
- Real men build rapport
- Perception is everything
- What is SELLING ?
  - o Sincere
  - o Engagement
  - o Looking
  - o Like you're
  - o Interested in
  - o Needs not
  - o Gain

Bryan McCormack

AND FINALLY...

I have to remind you of this final point - where most sellers go wrong is that they forget two vital things:

1. They are not in the selling business, they're in the people business.

2. They don't really understand what it is they're selling.

You're not just selling a product, you're selling yourself and your belief in that product, your conviction in it. You do not sell products, you sell solutions to problems and you meet needs. People want to own stuff and you are offering to help satisfy their desire to have it. That's a good thing.

How you make your customers feel is more important than what you sell them. Emotional attachments are powerful motivators and an emotional sale is always more mutually satisfying than an intellectual one.

So get out there and have fun with your sales character, the two of you are off on a journey of discovery that will take you places you've never been before both emotionally and financially. I've given you pretty much everything I can and now it's up to you to do something with it.

I wrote a book but what you do with what you've learned is up to you. So in closing I thought it would be useful to tell you the story of how this book that you're nearly finished reading came to be written:

Write Until You Get It Right

When Rintu suggested the idea for the book to me it was Sunday September 27th 2009. As I finish this final chapter it's getting on for one in the morning, December 27th. So everything that you've read up to this point has taken me roughly twelve weeks from start to finish. My lovely publisher is skiving, I'm sorry I mean taking a well-earned break until the third week in January. So that gives me another three weeks until I email her the completed manuscript and she can see just what it is she's signed up for! In those next three weeks I'll be doing what I've already been doing since I started: writing and re-writing until I get it right!

I started with the initial idea that Rintu gave me. My first task was to try and convince myself that I could do it and that I had enough to say. Then I came up with a title and sub-title. Next I wrote up my chapter titles and outlines. And then I listed everything that I wanted to say within those chapters. After that it was the easy bit - the actual writing! So I wrote chapter one, finished it and moved on to chapter two and finished that. Now this is where it gets interesting.

Before I wrote chapter three I went back and had another look at chapter one. That's when I noticed things I'd missed out, things that I could say more about, better ways of saying the same thing. I had an advantage I suppose in that I was used to this way of working from my time in the theatre where we were always looking for ways to improve what we had. If we had workshopped a play and improvised the material, in order to get something performable out of all that we then had to collate, write, review and then re-write. Several times. Often while on tour!

A play is an organic creation that is always developing and growing. If you have ever gone and seen the same show more than once you'll know what I'm talking about. Scripts in television are also notorious for being rewritten at the last minute and actors always dread the dreaded pink pages being pushed under their hotel door late at night. [Changes to a script are always made on different coloured paper so everyone knows what was changed when. Some scripts can resemble a rainbow by the time shooting finally ends!].

Dr Bryan Writeright

So now I moved on and wrote chapter four, then I went back and reviewed and rewrote chapter two and so on until I reached the end - which is where we are now! And why do I tell you this?

As a seller, you need to undertake the same review process for not just your sales technique but your entire life. Just like the rest of us.

I missed out terribly in the first half of my life by not having enough ambition, determination or knowledge. I thought that I had more than enough talent to succeed but as we've proved, *talent alone is not enough*. My goals? Well they were so nebulous as to be completely meaningless. I just wanted to keep working and be happy.

I ask you - what kind of a ridiculous goal is that to have for your life?

The less well-defined your goals are, the more nebulous and fuzzy they are, the more general they are, the less specific they are, the less likely you are to ever achieve them. I know that to my cost and as a result the first half of my life has been less enjoyable and fulfilling than it should have or could have been. Don't make my mistake. Please.

As either a seller or an actor, every day of your life, both inside and outside of your work, you should always be looking to constantly, consistently and continuously improve. The Japanese have a word for it - kaizen - and it's allied to this concept:

Know Yourself...

You must know who you really are and why you are here. You must know what your purpose is for being alive and you must have a plan for how you're going to achieve it. You need to stay flexible enough to be able to adapt to unforeseen obstacles you may encounter along the way.

Above all you must be prepared to do *whatever it takes* to achieve your goals and those goals must be specific. Get it? Got it? Good!

You shouldn't be in sales unless selling is wired into your DNA like acting is in mine. If you don't love it to the exclusion of all else, if it's just an enjoyable job to pay the bills, then take my advice and get out now.

While you still can. Too many people compromise in life and end up trapped in a well-paid job that they don't enjoy. The best job in the world is the one you love doing and for me that's acting and everything related to it. If selling's not like that for you - stop doing it!

Your sales character is just a natural extension of yourself but the really smart ones amongst you will have already realised that you can create a character for yourself in any area of your life, not just sales. You can use that character to grow yourself into who you ultimately want to become, you can use him to shield yourself from the toxic effects of rejection and SBDs. And now that you've read this book, you and you alone are the one who can take the actions that need to be taken to make the most of all the new knowledge that you've gained.

From now on, your ultimate aim for what's left of your life should be this - don't just aim to become The Best Seller You Can Be, no, aim higher my friend. Aim to become The Best You That You Can Be!

It's my sincere hope that this book has helped you to see that you can achieve that. Now it's up to you to get out there and make it happen.

Go have a happy life and act your way to success.

You've been a great audience! Thank You and Goodnight!

And for my first encore...

Bryan McCormack

Hamlet – Act 3, Scene 2

[Poor old Hammie instructs the players]

Speak the speech, I pray you, as I pronounced it to you, trippingly on the tongue: use all gently, for in the very torrent, tempest, and whirlwind of passion, you must acquire and beget a temperance that may give it smoothness. Be not too tame neither, suit the action to the word, the word to the action; with this special o'erstep not the modesty of nature: for any thing so overdone is from the purpose of playing, whose end, both at the first and now, was and is, to hold, as 'twere, the mirror up to nature; to show virtue her own feature, scorn her own image, and the very age and body of the time his form and pressure. Now this overdone, or come tardy off, though it make the unskilful laugh, cannot but make the judicious grieve.

O, there be players that I have seen play, and heard others praise, and that highly, not to speak it profanely, that have so strutted and bellowed that I have thought some of nature's journeymen had made men and not made them well, they imitated humanity so abominably. And let those that play your clowns speak no more than is set down for them; for there be of them that will themselves laugh, to set on some quantity of barren spectators to laugh too; though, in the mean time, some necessary question of the play be then to be considered: that's villainous, and shows a most pitiful ambition in the fool that uses it. Go, make you ready.

CURTAIN DOWN!

1. INT. THE THEATRE.

Our Hero leaves the stage as RAPTUROUS APPLAUSE continues. Then, from the PA System:

ANNOUNCER: Ladies and Gentlemen, thank you for attending tonight's performance of "Sell Your Self: Act Your Way To Sales Success", which has now concluded. Mr McCormack will be signing copies of his book in the theatre foyer shortly. Please form an orderly queue.

The AUDIENCE slowly begin to file out, some making their way to the THEATRE BAR, most to the FOYER.

2. INT. DRESSING ROOM.

Our Hero ENTERS to find a bouquet of flowers on his dressing room table. He takes off his jacket and SMILES at the message on the card: "Well done on another great show!"

3. INT. THEATRE FOYER

The AUDIENCE are BUYING their copies of THE BOOK and begin to queue, EXCITED as they wait for Our Hero to appear.

Foyer Steadicam - stand by please for closing shots

4. INT. DRESSING ROOM.

Our Hero has changed his clothes. He checks his pockets - plenty of BUSINESS CARDS & two PENS [just in case]. With a final look in the mirror, he is ready for the rest of the show and EXITS.

5. INT. THEATRE FOYER.

The AUDIENCE CHEER as Our Hero APPEARS! He acknowledges his public as he settles himself behind the table. He reaches out and shakes the hand of the FIRST PERSON in the queue:

HERO: Hello there! I'm Bryan McCormack, thanks for coming tonight! So, what did you think of the show?

And TX Out...

Thank you everyone, that's a wrap!

AND... ROLL THE CREDITS!

As previously stated, my thanks go first and foremost to *that very nice man* from the foreword, Mr Rintu Basu. Not just for giving me the idea in the first place but for all his support, help and advice. A better friend and mentor and guide through the minefield of writing your first book I could not have hoped for and I couldn't have done it without him.

After Rintu the next person who deserves my thanks is without doubt my publisher, the lovely Debbie Jenkins, for only taking three days to say yes!

And finally my thanks go to you, dear reader. Thank you for helping me in my ongoing efforts to keep my cat in the manner to which he soon hopes to become accustomed! [Unless of course you're a cheapskate who's reading someone else's copy. Go buy your own!]

I hope this has been as much fun for you to read as it was for me to write and as a thank you for buying my first book there's some stuff that I want to give you...

BEFORE I GO...

...if you head on over to:

www.actyourwayto.com

...you'll get access to some great free stuff, my thank you to you for buying this book. And when you've done that, subscribe to my blog and keep in touch. You can stay up to date with all my latest articles on acting and selling, get advance notice on future books and products and all sorts of good stuff that I couldn't fit into this book!

I look forward to hearing from you and helping you in any way I can.

Thanks for reading and I wish you every success as you go out there, take what you've learned and Sell Your Self!

[And don't forget to let me know how you get on, OK? Ciao for now!]

If You Have Enjoyed THIS Book...

...then here are some others that I think you will enjoy too!

THE WEALTHY AUTHOR by Debbie Jenkins and Joe Gregory
(www.publishingacademy.com)

The book that tells you how to do what I've just done!

PERSUASION SKILLS BLACK BOOK by Rintu Basu
(www.bookshaker.com)

Written by my good friend that very nice man. Visit his website at www.thenlpcompany.com

SELLING TO WIN by Richard Denny (www.kogan-page.co.uk)

The first book on selling I ever bought and the one I keep going back to again and again. A classic.

BARE KNUCKLE SELLING and BARE KNUCKLE NEGOTIATING by Simon Hazeldine (www.bookshaker.com)

Simon Hazeldine's streetwise guide to selling and negotiating, based on his many years as a top sales trainer.

Persuasion
Skills

BLACK BOOK

Practical NLP Language Patterns for
Getting The Response You Want

Rintu Basu

FREE INSIDE
'Black Book'
Persuasion
Training
E-course

com

BARE KNUCKLE
SELLING

KNOCKOUT SALES TACTICS THEY WON'T
TEACH YOU AT BUSINESS SCHOOL

SIMON HAZELDINE
FOREWORD BY DR. JOE VITALE

om

BARE KNUCKLE
NEGOTIATING

KNOCKOUT NEGOTIATION TACTICS THEY
WON'T TEACH YOU AT BUSINESS SCHOOL

Download
FREE
'Bare Knuckle'
Bonuses

SIMON HAZELDINE
FOREWORD BY DUNCAN BANNATYNE OBE
from BBC TV's "Dragons' Den"

om

Lightning Source UK Ltd.
Milton Keynes UK
31 August 2010

159228UK00001B/3/P